Soups, Stews & Stories:

**An investigative reporter's
global quest to nourish the soul**

Early Praise for *Soups, Stews & Stories: An investigative reporter's global quest to nourish the soul*

"Set aside a little extra time when you're cooking from this book—as you will want to do immediately—because you're bound to get enmeshed in the great stories it contains."

—David McCumber: author, Lee Enterprises Local News Director for the American West, former Washington bureau chief for Hearst Newspapers

"With his formidable culinary instincts, Andy Schneider could have been a star professional chef. He chose instead to become a premier investigative journalist, one whose stories changed laws and saved lives, and saved his kitchen creations for those of us fortunate enough to be his friends. In this book, Andy's two passions come together: exquisite recipes, made all the more delicious by the tales of their discovery. Now, everyone can experience the magic of Andy's table."

—David Boardman, former editor of *The Seattle Times*, editor of multiple Pulitzer-Prize-winning investigations and currently dean of Klein College of Media and Communication at Temple University

"I worked closely with Andrew Schneider for many years, and let me tell you; it wasn't easy. The food, however, always made it worthwhile. Herein is a lifetime of recipes and stories served best with those you want to stay friends with."

—Vincent J. Musi, author of *The Year of the Dogs*

Soups, Stews & Stories:

An investigative reporter's global quest to nourish the soul

By Andrew Schneider and Kathleen Best

New Bay Books

SOUPS, STEWS & STORIES:
An investigative reporter's global quest to nourish the soul

By Andrew Schneider
and Kathleen Best

Edited by William Lambrecht and Sandra Olivetti Martin
with Felix Tower

Copyright © 2022
by Kathleen Best
All Rights Reserved

New Bay Books
Fairhaven, Maryland • NewBayBooks@gmail.com

Design by Suzanne Shelden
Shelden Studios
Prince Frederick, Maryland • sheldenstudios@comcast.net

Cover Photo: Andy shops at Pike Place Market. Photo by Paul Kitagaki Jr.
and background "Ingredients" photograph by Andrew Schneider
Section Headers and Flyleaf Art: A collage of Andrew Schneider's press
credentials covering five decades. Photo by Kurt Wilson

A Note on Type:
Cover and section heads are set in Al Fresco Script
Text font is Garamond Premier Pro

Library of Congress
Cataloging-in-Publication Data
979-8-9853477-4-6
Printed in the United States of America
First Edition

Dedication

To Andy, who made me laugh,
made me plump and made me believe
I could do anything, even cook.

Andy and Kathy. Photo by Vincent J. Musi

Foreword

Andy was a beacon to a generation of hard-charging journalists, and a friend. He delivered the kind of crusading prose Upton Sinclair pioneered a century before. Environmental journalists are a broad lot, with many devoted to policy and regulation. Others chronicle threats to flora and fauna. Just about everybody in the field is engulfed in the deepening climate crisis.

Andy's environmental journalism was a brand unto itself, an uncompromising focus on health on behalf of the victims of sins against nature.

I became aware of Andy's work when, as an Associated Press reporter in New England decades ago, he documented hazardous waste. Those stories earned him a beating from thugs. You'll read about this and other times he confronted the purveyors of poison in this book's introduction, by Kathy Best, his wife and journalism soul-mate.

I remain awed by Andy's stories in the *Seattle Post-Intelligencer* and a book about the tragic asbestos contamination in Libby, Montana, a tale of betrayal of a community by a corporation, the Environmental Protection Agency and even the local medical establishment.

Andy had a theory about investigative journalism: "Every good story has a villain." The Montana villain was W.R. Grace, the chemicals giant that federal prosecutors said made more than 1,000 people sick from contamination. Many people died.

I had the good fortune of working with Andy at the *St. Louis Post-Dispatch*, me in Washington and him in the newsroom. I recall the words from a St. Louis editor a few months after he'd joined the paper: "You were right. Schneider is a force of nature."

Andy also was a force in the kitchen, as you'll see in his painstaking assembling of recipes from around the world, many gathered while he was on assignment. To Andy, food was a salve for the vicissitudes of life, a time for friends and celebration.

He was joyful and full of stories in his artfully appointed kitchens. I recall eating with him at restaurants from Annapolis to Seattle. The son of a maitre d', Andy was disappointed by substandard fare. (The only dish at our house he spurned was shad roe. Fish eggs are an acquired taste.)

At a tony Missoula bistro, he was troubled by the skimpy paté on a charcuterie board he judged lame. I cheered him with a tale from our just-completed canoe journey, through the White Cliffs of the Upper Missouri River Breaks National Monument.

The trip was semi-glamping, comfortable tents ready for paddlers and chuck wagons with plenty of liquor. Around the campfire one night, a fellow in our party remarked that he had retired not long ago from W.R. Grace, which recently had come out of bankruptcy—forced by Andy's stories—a healthier company.

I asked (politely) if he happened to have read a book by friends of mine, Andy Schneider and David McCumber, in which his company featured prominently.

"No. What's it called?" he asked.

Why, on a three-day watery excursion, I had packed a hardcopy version of a book I'd already read, I can't say. Andy howled with laughter as I recounted how, in the dark, I took a shortcut to our tent through a pasture full of snoozing cows—and many cow pies.

I handed the ex-Grace executive the book: *An Air that Kills: How the Asbestos Poisoning of Libby, Montana Uncovered a National Scandal.*

"You should read this," I said.

I offer the same advice for this collection of recipes assembled by a lover of food and a master in the art of journalism.

At our fledgling publishing house, Sandra Olivetti Martin and I are grateful for the opportunity to bring Andrew Schneider's cookbook to life.

—William Lambrecht, editor
New Bay Books

Introduction

"Andy Schneider was the best goddam friend that those without friends could have."

Of all the tributes to Andy's reporting career that poured in after his death, in 2017, those words from Mike Harbut, one of the top pulmonologists in the U.S. and the medical adviser to Polish President Lech Walesa, came the closest to capturing the man I shared my life with for a quarter-century. They would have meant more to him than the closet full of awards, including two Pulitzers, that he earned.

Schneider, right, celebrates with Pittsburgh Press colleagues Matthew Brelis and Vince Musi, holding the phone, after they won the Pulitzer Prize for Public Service for revealing the FAA's failure to adequately screen airline pilots for drugs, alcohol and other medical conditions. Photo by Bill Wade, Pittsburgh Press

He didn't come from privilege, so he chose to focus his investigations on those without power.

A 14-year-old Haitian girl who came home from a trip to Port-au-Prince with $40 and a scar where one of her kidneys used to be. Miners and their families poisoned by asbestos in Libby, Montana, that W.R. Grace knew was in the ore but hid from them. A Navy reservist dragged to the jungles of Bolivia to fight America's secret war on drugs and the commanders who admitted the mission was a mess. A Red Cross worker in Elba, Alabama, betrayed by her organization when a burst dam inundated her town. All talked to Andy because they knew he cared about them and would do what it took to tell their stories.

He had the scars to prove it. In Haiti, his thumbs were broken and he was hacked with a machete by the Tonton Macoute, the vicious paramilitary organization created by the Duvalier regimes. When he backed into a devil thorn bush, a voodoo priest with a medical degree from Tulane University healed his wounds. His mother learned he had been shot in the Dominican Republic when she saw a photo of him running across a square in the pages of the *Miami Herald*. When he asked too many questions about illegal toxic waste dumping in New England, he was stabbed with an ice pick, becoming the subject of a story by his own employer at the time, The Associated Press.

These were stories he didn't tell many, preferring to focus on the travails of others. In doing so, he made the nation's organ transplant system fairer by helping ensure that the miner's daughter got the same shot at a heart as the Saudi sultan. He made flying safer by disclosing that the medical screening of pilots for drugs and alcohol was inadequate. He got out of jail innocent people who had been wrongly accused of participating in a child sex ring. And he shone a light on unsafe railroad bridges, tainted honey and the dangers of nanoparticles in consumer products, among other stories in a career that spanned more than five decades.

The work didn't make him cynical. Andy's joy for life was too infectious. Unless you were corrupt or incompetent, resistance to his charm was futile. His personality filled a room when he entered it. His embrace of friends—decades old and those he'd just met—was irresistible.

Then there was the food.

I don't know when this love affair began, but I suspect it was in childhood. Andy's father, who emigrated from Hungary as a young teen, went to culinary school after being drafted into the U.S. Army in World War II. His mother learned her kitchen skills from her husband but also from her grandmother, Andy's Bubbe, who owned restaurants in Brooklyn and New Haven, Connecticut, where she fed struggling performers, Jimmy Durante among them, for free after hours.

In the Jewish tradition, food was love. And he was very well loved by adoring aunts, a mother, grandmother and great-grandmother who all lived together in the Hiawatha Apartments in Miami Beach while his father was in the Army and stuffed him with goodies at every opportunity.

Schneider sits in the lap of his mother, Frances, surrounded by adoring aunts on Miami Beach in this 1943 family photo.

No wonder, then, that the kitchen was always Andy's happy place.

Stocking it gave him almost as much joy as cooking in it. There was never a quick trip to the grocery store. Andy was a tactile shopper, especially in markets. He *needed* to caress the salmon, sniff the paprika, squeeze the porcini, heft the fennel, inspect the lobster. He would run his hands along the shelves as he stalked every aisle in search of new and interesting ingredients. (This explains why many of the recipes in this book have A LOT of ingredients.) And, of course, he would engage the purveyors in conversation, interviewing them about what's new, what's fresh, what makes an interesting preparation, acquiring new friends as he went.

Those friendships paid off more than once when he lived on Capitol Hill in Washington, D.C., had invited a houseful to dinner but a key interview robbed him of time to shop. He'd call his favorite butcher at Eastern Market, place orders for vegetables, cheese, meat and pasta, and pick up the bagged and boxed provisions on his way home—a service not provided to everyone.

Years after leaving Washington, D.C., Andy still relished visits to his favorite Eastern Market vendor, who took him behind the counter to see (and sniff) the latest products. Photo by Paul Kitagaki Jr.

And oh, those dinners.

First as an Army photographer, then as a reporter, Andy traveled the world. As he collected facts and photos, so he collected recipes. Hundreds of them. Lamb in Christchurch, New Zealand. Black ice lobster in Sherbrooke, Quebec. Wild mushroom soup in the Deschutes National Forest of Oregon. Hurricane vegetable paella in Homestead, Florida. Map Debat patriot stew in Port-au-Prince, Haiti.

When Andy cooked, the air was redolent of herbs, spices, browning butter and searing meat.

His descriptions of the kitchen's sounds and smells could border on the religious. "You must stir the roux constantly," he wrote, "never leaving the pot, not to pee, yell at the dogs or answer the door, until the roux is a dark, rich mahogany or chocolate in color. Anticipate a wonderful aroma when the roux is nearly just perfect ...You could be looking at about 30 minutes depending on the heat. It seems to go faster with zydeco playing in the background."

Bowls, cutting boards, pots, pans, jars, bottles, broth cans—most painted in sauces and juices—littered the counters before dinner was served. Andy appeared to believe that the bigger the mess, the better the meal, especially if, borrowing from Tom Sawyer, he had friends around willing to clean up after him.

The dishes Andy collected were delicious, of course. But the stories that inspired them were delectable. Although he only got around to writing down a fraction of them—he had planned to publish this cookbook later—he shared them like condiments when guests remarked on a serving.

So welcome to Andy's table. Pull up a chair. Enjoy some good stories and some good food.

—Kathy Best

P.S. Andy constantly experimented with his recipes. The many friends and cooks who have tested these recipes suggest you follow your inspiration as you cook them.

Raising a toast to the latest meal are, from left, Erin Loos Cutraro, Schneider, Vince Musi and Callie Shell. Photo by Andrew Cutraro

Schneider's battered typewriter case traveled on assignments around the world, helping him write captions in the days before computers. Photo by Kathy Best

Contents

I. The Caribbean

The Bahamas
    Caribbean Seafood Paella 7
    French Nuns' Vegetable Soup 10
    Red Snapper with Bimini Mango Salsa 13

Cuba
    The Chili Formerly Known as Guantanamo 17

Dominican Republic
    Invasion Mango Flan 21

Florida
    Flamingo Grilled Shrimp 24
    Hurricane Vegetable Paella 29

Haiti
    Map Debat Patriot Stew 33
    Armando's Cuban Pork 36

II. Latin America

Bolivia
    Cochabamba Steak With Ginger Marinade 44

Ecuador
    Ecuadorian Citrus Shrimp Soup 46
    Rio Coca Amazonian Gazpacho 49

Panama
    Tarragon and Fennel Soup 52

III. The American South

Alabama
    Moses' Porkin' Heaven Rub 59

Georgia
    Gandy Dancer Dirty Rice 61

Louisiana
    Everyman's Gumbo 64

North Carolina
    Preacher's Red-Eye Gravy 68

South Carolina
    And God Said "Country Ham" 70
    Blindman's Grits and Ham 74
    Shrimp and Grits 76

IV. Chesapeake Country

Maryland
    A Great Teacher's Chesapeake Fish Stew 84
    Salt Spray Basil and Tomato Soup 87

Maryland's Eastern Shore
    Saffron Crab Soup 89

Washington D.C.
    Gorgonzola and Celery Soup 92
    Mo Udall's Old Senate Bean Soup 94

V. The Northeast

Maine
    Screw the Admiral Lobster Stew 103

New Hampshire
    Civil War Baked Beans 107
    Milne's Lobster Stew 111
    Miss Lillian's Peanut Soup 114
    Pot Roast Au Vin 118

Quebec
    Black Ice Lobster Quebec 121
    Coq au Vin Pacific 123

VI. The Northwest

Montana
    Duck Breasts with Huckleberry Sauce 133
    A Montana Standing Prime Rib Roast 137

Oregon
    Fog-Bound Spinach Soup 139
    Forest Wild Mushroom Soup 141
    Scallop Confetti Soup 146

Washington State
    D.B. Cooper Salmon Hash 149
    Doctor Daughter's Poached Salmon 151

VII. Far and Wide

Italy
    Essence of Italy Soup 161
    Great Italian Grain Salad 165
    It's Really Not Italian Wedding Soup 168
    Pasta Carbonara with Pancetta and Prosciutto 171

Japan
    Dried and Fresh Shiitake Cure-All Soup 173

Lebanon
    Beirut Lentil Soup 175

New Zealand
    Christ Church Leg of Lamb 178
    Shanks of a Suspected Spy 181

VIII. At Home

Soup
    Hungarian Cauliflower Soup 190

Sides
    Bubbe's Latkes 193
    Good Morning Biscuits and Sausage Gravy 195
    Fried Green Tomatoes 197
    Southern Surprise Cornbread Dressing 199
    Walla Walla Sweet Onion Pie 203
    "What am I, chopped liver?" 205

Sweets
    Patrick's Cranberry Experiment 207
    Holiday Hazelnut Brittle 208

I

The Caribbean

1959-1995

Schneider savors a daiquiri on the patio of the Hotel Nacional de Cuba in Havana in 2014, a month before President Barack Obama began to normalize relations with the Caribbean island. Photo by Kathy Best

The Caribbean

Andy didn't graduate from the technical high school he attended in Miami, although he went on to attend college and graduate school and hold a distinguished chair in journalism at Indiana University.

The reason for his checkered education? His love of photography and storytelling. His high school's photo class was taught by a former *Life* magazine photo editor who required his students to produce magazine-style photo spreads. Inspired by his teacher's work, Andy headed to the mountains of Cuba in his senior year to photograph the band of rebels he'd been reading so much about: Fidel Castro and his followers.

He found them and talked his way into their camp. (Tragically, his negatives were later lost.) But he also got hepatitis and missed a chunk of his senior year, eventually earning a GED that let him enroll in classes at the University of Maryland when he was in the Army and, later, the University of Massachusetts at Lowell.

Hepatitis wasn't the only bug he picked up in Cuba. Journalism and a love for the Caribbean had entered his bloodstream.

He took pictures throughout the region for the tiny Caribbean International News Service based in an office in Nassau, Bahamas, across the street from a liquor store and next door to a convent school. The girls, many from wealthy European families, would climb over the wall at night to drink and listen to music played by his roommates, including a gifted drummer named Peanuts.

Andy graduated to United Press International, covering the failed plots by Cuban ex-pats in Florida to retake their country from Castro in the early 1960s, the bloody 1964 assault on civil rights protesters in St. Augustine, Florida, the U.S. invasion to put down a 1965 coup attempt in the Dominican Republic, several Apollo moon shots and the internment at Guantanamo Bay of refugees who tried but failed to reach American shores.

His coverage of Gitmo produced a chili that won newsroom competitions from coast to coast. The recipe resulted from the chance meeting of a GI from Georgia, whose family sent him home from leave with a smoked pork butt, and a doctor's family held at Guantanamo after their attempt to flee Castro's Cuba failed. The soldier and the prisoners joined forces to create a green pork chili with mango, tomatillos and Caribbean spices that cannot be beat.

Andy's most enduring Caribbean infatuation, however, was with Haiti, a place he returned to again and again for at least four different news organizations.

Schneider takes notes in Port-au-Prince, Haiti, in September 1994.

He covered the jubilation of tens of thousands of Haitians when President-for-life Jean-Claude "Baby Doc" Duvalier fled the country in 1986. He uncovered with *Pittsburgh Press* colleague Mary Pat

Flaherty the black-market trade in human organs that won his first Pulitzer Prize. And he witnessed the 1994 invasion by U.S. troops to restore the presidency of Jean-Bertrand Aristide, Haiti's first democratically elected president, who had been toppled in a coup in 1990.

He loved the people, befriending a voodoo priest who had earned his medical degree at Tulane University, returned to Haiti to help his people and became a source for life. He loved the culture, filling the house with Haitian art. And, of course, he loved the food.

Map Debat Patriot Stew is a recipe he put together after watching the celebration of Baby Doc's ouster.

—Kathy Best

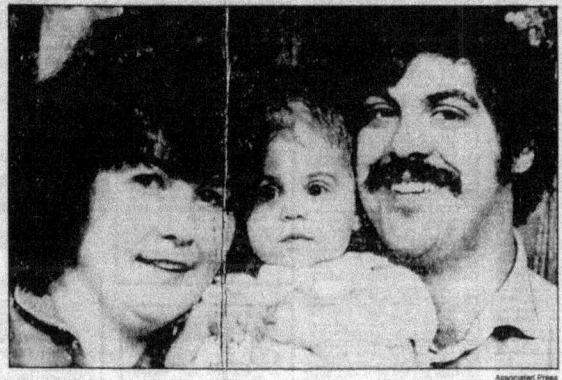

The Caribbean

The Bahamas
Caribbean Seafood Paella
French Nuns' Vegetable Soup
Red Snapper with Bimini Mango Salsa

Cuba
The Chili Formerly Known as Guantanamo

Dominican Republic
Invasion Mango Flan

Florida
Flamingo Grilled Shrimp
Hurricane Vegetable Paella

Haiti
Map Debat Patriot Stew
Armando's Cuban Pork

The Bahamas   Caribbean Seafood Paella

This recipe is an adaptation from Carmela Salaha, a wonderful, spicy lady who came to Nassau in the 1960s from Valencia, Spain.

Carmela brought with her not only a love for seafood but also the first paellera to the Bahamian Island. This uniquely designed paella pan is wide, round, and only 1½ to 2 inches deep. It has splayed sides and two looped handles. The pan is designed to allow the rice base to be spread thinly and, if the cook is skillful, produce a golden caramelized crust of rice across the bottom of the pan.

Valencian paella usually centers on two basic flavors, either meat or fish. But Carmela, perhaps in deference to the Italian-born Conga drummer with whom she was living, added sausage and spiced ham to the small but tasty Lagosta or Bahamian lobster, shrimp and other shellfish.

Saffron is vital to the flavor, but sofrito, a gently cooked blend of tomato, garlic, and onion, gives any paella its heart.

I suggest you use sea scallops for this recipe. They are about 1 ½-inch in diameter and are a little chewier than the smaller Bay scallops, but they're sweet and their larger size works well in this paella. Lagosta or Bahamian crayfish are small lobsters, about a half-pound each, and are now being sold in many fish markets.

Above: Seafood paella cooks in the pan. Photo by Andrew Schneider

Ingredients for 8 servings

Small lobsters	3
Olive oil, extra virgin	2 T
Sea scallops, halved	¾ lb.
Chorizo sausage cut in ½" pieces	2
Salvadoran or mild Italian sausages	3
Tasso, cut in ½" cubes	½ lb
Spanish or red onions, cut in ½" pieces	2 medium
Garlic, shaved	2 cloves
Green pepper, cut in ½" pieces	1
Sweet red or yellow peppers, cut in ½" pieces	2
Roma tomato, sliced ¼" thick	4
Chopped tomatoes in juice	1 lb.
Artichoke hearts, cut in half	5 oz.
Kosher salt	½ t
White pepper	½ t
Old Bay seasoning	2 t
Paella rice (or Arborio or other short-grain rice)	2½ cups
Saffron threads, toasted	½ t
Chicken or fish stock	1¼ quarts
Mango, cubed ½"	1½ cups

Optional

Cornish game hens, cut into 4 pieces each	3 small

Cook lobster or crayfish. Chill and separate tails and claws, remove shells and set meat aside. Cut game hens, if using, and set aside.

Over a medium flame, heat olive oil in a paella pan (or large skillet).

Add sausage and Tasso and sauté until browned; remove and set aside. Add game hen and sauté until brown; remove and set aside.

Add scallops and brown 45-60 seconds on each side. Remove from pan. Add lobster, stir and cook another minute and remove from pan and set aside.

Add onions and sauté until light brown. Add minced garlic and peppers. Cook for three minutes and lower heat. Add sliced Roma and chopped cooked tomatoes, artichokes, and seasonings. Stir gently and cook for 5 minutes.

Add rice. Stir to coat the rice grains with the oil. Add toasted saffron to ¼ cup hot chicken or fish stock and add to pan. Add chicken and sausage; stir gently.

Add remainder of stock and bring to boil, lower heat, do not stir. Cook until rice is almost done, about 15 minutes. Add seafood and mango. Cook about 5 more minutes until rice is done. Remove from heat, cover with foil and let rest 10 minutes.

"Soooooo good!" said test chef Cindy Shearer.

The Bahamas — French Nuns' Vegetable Soup

This recipe is like a French minestrone dotted with cold pesto. It was adapted from the cook for a fascinating gaggle of French nuns whose convent bordered my yard when I worked in Nassau, in the Bahamas. What vegetables they couldn't grow themselves to make the Soupe au Pistou, they bartered from the kitchen help in the restaurants on Bay Street or visiting tour ships.

Above: French Nuns' Vegetable Soup. Photo by Kathy Best

Ingredients for 10 1-cup servings

For the soup

Bacon or pork fat back, cut 1" thick	3 slices
Green beans, sliced thin	½ lb.
Leeks, tipped and sliced thin	½ lb.
Fennel, sliced thin	1 cup
Celery, sliced thin	3 stalks
Carrots, sliced thin	2 medium
Small red potatoes, quartered	1 lb.
Zucchini, cut in ½" slices	2 medium
Yellow squash, cut in ½" slices	2 medium
Tomato, diced	1 large
Olive oil	2 t
Chicken or vegetable broth	10 cups
Orzo	⅓ cup
Herbs de Provence	1 T
Salt and pepper to taste	

In a heavy-bottom pot, cook bacon or pork until mostly crisp. Remove, retaining the fat.

Clean and slice the vegetables. Add the olive oil to the pork fat and sauté vegetables over medium heat until the potatoes and carrots start to get a little tender. Then add the chicken broth, the herbs de Provence and a bit of Kosher salt and white pepper, and cover. Simmer over medium-low heat for about 30 minutes, or until the potatoes can be pierced with a fork. Add the pieces of cooked pork.

Add the orzo or any other tiny pasta of choice. Bring the mixture to a boil and cook until the pasta is cooked through.

Taste and adjust the seasonings.

For the Pistou

Cilantro, basil, or parsley, chopped	2 cups
Garlic, minced	4 cloves
Extra virgin olive oil	¼ cup
Salt and pepper to taste	

Optional

Parmigiano Reggiano or similar hard cheese	2 oz.

To make this French version of cold pesto without nuts or cheese, cilantro or parsley can be used, as can the traditional basil, which is my personal third choice. Mix herbs with olive oil and add salt, white pepper and garlic. Combine all ingredients into a mortar and use the pestle to force the blend into a smooth paste. Or if traditional means little, add ingredients into a food processor and blend until you reach the texture you desire.

Should you wish to add cheese, I suggest a healthy Parmesan, Romano, Asiago, pecorino or any other flavorful hard cheese.

Serve this hearty soup in large bowls topped with a healthy spoonful of the pistou.

The Bahamas — Red Snapper with Bimini Mango Salsa

Adapted from a memory of snapper served in Bimini decades ago.

Bimini is a tiny Bahamian Island 50 miles from Miami. Today there are the same hotels, resorts and trendy boutiques that conceal the heart of almost every island in the Caribbean. Decades ago, before tourists became bored with Nassau and drug runners were avoiding the Bahamian authorities instead of buying them, the nine-mile-long spit of sand known as Bimini was the home to real fishers, both commercial and sport. The two hotels in Alicetown were tiny but authentic down to the 16 types of flavored rum served in the beachside bars.

Above: Red Snapper with Bimini Mango Salsa. Photo by Jim Shearer

Ingredients for four servings

Salsa

Mango, cut in ½" pieces	1½ cups
Pink grapefruit or orange, cut in ¼" pieces	1 cup
Red onion, chopped fine	2 T
Green onion, chopped fine	2 T
Lime or lemon juice	3 T
Orange zest	1 T
Red pepper, chopped fine	½ large
Cilantro, chopped fine	2 T
Orange juice	¼ cup
Old Bay seafood seasoning	1 t
Smoked chile powder	½ t

Fish

Red snapper filets, about 8 oz., pin bones removed	4
Eggs, beaten	2
Salt and pepper to taste	
Flour	¼ cup
Fine corn meal or fine breadcrumbs	½ cup
Peanut oil	4 T

Combine the ingredients and seasonings for the salsa. Cover and refrigerate for 1-4 hours.

Heat the salsa in a separate pan over medium heat until first sign of boiling, then turn down heat to low simmer.

Beat the eggs. Mix the flour, breadcrumbs and salt and pepper. Dip the fish into the egg mixture, then dredge in mixture of flour and breadcrumbs.

Heat oil in a sauté pan large enough to permit the filets to lay flat. If you must cook the fish in two batches, preheat the oven to 275 degrees to keep the fish warm.

Cook the filets over medium high heat about 3 or 4 minutes on one side and a minute or two on the other, depending on thickness. (If using a meat thermometer, the filets should reach 145 degrees.) The fish should be a crisp, golden brown.

Serve beneath hot salsa.

Guantanamo: Schneider prepares red onions in his Des Moines, Washington, kitchen. Photo by Paul Kitagaki Jr.

Cuba The Chili Formerly Known as Guantanamo

Guantanamo Bay, Cuba – Since 1903, long before it became a controversial prison for alleged terrorists, Guantanamo Naval Station on Cuba's southeastern tip of Oriente province was a tropical country-club hideaway for the U.S. military. It also was a refugee camp for thousands fleeing Caribbean dictators captured before reaching American shores. In the 1980s and '90s, the 45-square-mile "GTMO" was home to as many as 8,000 men, women and children—about a 50-50 split of Haitians fleeing Baby Doc Duvalier and Cubans running from Fidel—all stopped shy of South Florida by U.S. forces.

While the diplomats and politicians debated what to do with these boaters to freedom, their day-to-day care and survival fell to 225 GIs, who patrolled the red-dirt-packed streets and rows of dusty tents that made up the hastily assembled city.

The GIs and the refugees had something in common. Neither wanted to be there. For the most part, it was a congenial arrangement, and the young guards, mostly in their late teens and early 20s, did what they could to help those trapped by the government inertia.

William Black, a tall, spit-and-polish military policeman from South Georgia, cautiously befriended one Cuban family, Roberto and his wife—both physicians—and their three almost grown daughters. The soldier, in his limited Spanish, talked music with the girls and baseball and food with their parents. The 21-year-old tried to explain that he came from a family of cooks, that his father, uncle and grandfather all knew their barbeque and "how to make a hunk of pork sing."

"Ah, el puerco," the physician beamed. And with the help of a bilingual chaplain, he explained that they would grill a pig when they could get one, sewing spices, chiles and fruit into the belly of the porker as it cooked. Black talked about the spices, the dry rubs, his family used at home. He tried to explain how they slowly cooked the pork over aromatic wood like cherry, peach, apple and hickory.

But talking about wonderful, home-cooked meals when rice, beans and military rations made up the bulk of the daily menu did little for anyone's morale.

That changed when Black went home to Georgia for a week-long leave. He smuggled back onto this island, 400 air miles from Miami, a triple-wrapped, 12-pound pork butt, fresh from his family's smoker. Quickly Roberto and his wife scrounged up local spices, chiles and fruit, and a cultural culinary summit was convened around a well-scrubbed, aged iron kettle. The blissful result was called Gitmo Green. If it were not for the addition of Caribbean favorites of mango, lime and orange, this refugee camp special would come close to the classic Chili Verde.

Ingredients for 20 servings

Pork butt, smoked, cut into ¾" cubes	7½ lbs.
Green chiles, mild, charred, seeded, and diced	8
Red sweet peppers, cut into ½" squares	5 large
Green peppers, cut into ½" squares	5 large
Peanut or olive oil	7 oz.
Red onions, cut into ½" squares	5 large
Garlic, shaved or minced	20 cloves
Tomatillos, sliced ⅓" thick	15
Roma tomatoes, sliced ⅓" thick	15
Pasilla chiles, dried and smoked, powdered,	2
Basil, dried	3 T
Smoked paprika	2 T
Kosher salt	3 T
Lemon pepper	2 T

Cumin powder	1 T
Mustard seed, yellow	2 T
Orange juice	8 T
Flour	5 T
Vinegar, cider, or white wine	6 T
Chicken or beef broth	6 cups
Mangos, peeled and chopped into large pieces	3
Lime zest	1 t
Lime juice	2 T
Mexican oregano, dried	3 T
Tortillas, flour	40 8"
Brown or white rice, on the side	
To garnish	
Green onions, chopped ¼"	4
Cilantro, washed, dried, and chopped	1 bunch

The key to this recipe is the hunk of well-seasoned pork butt or loin, smoked, if possible, but in any case, cooked until it's almost fall-apart-tender, cooled, cut into ¾" cubes and set aside. (See my recipe for Porkin' Heaven Rub for the dry rub I use on many pork dishes and for instructions on how to marinate and prepare pork butt.)

Roast the chiles and peppers over fire or a gas burner until skin is charred. Place in bag until cool; then remove the charred skin, stem, and seeds.

In a large heavy-bottom pan, heat peanut or olive oil over medium heat and add red onion. Cook for 10 minutes until soft.

Add garlic, tomatillos, tomatoes, and peppers. Stir and cook 15 minutes. Add chiles and seasonings and cook another 15 minutes.

Mix half the orange juice and flour. Add to pan with vinegar and stock and stir well; add pork and bring mixture to a light boil. Cover and simmer until pork is tender, usually for 45 minutes to 90 minutes, stirring frequently.

Add mango, lime zest, and remaining juice. Cook until the fruit is soft. Taste and adjust seasonings.

Top with green onions and/or cilantro. Serve with rice and tortillas.

Notes on chiles

According to Roberto, you select your chiles depending on how much you love or hate the people you're feeding. With chiles, there comes a point where the seasonings are not just hot but uncomfortable. You don't want that degree of intensity unless you're trying to show that your daughter's suitor is a wimp, the Cuban pediatrician explained, dropping his voice to a whisper so the ladies of his family wouldn't hear.

My favorite for this recipe is the careful addition of a bit of smoked pasilla, or chile negro as it's called when dried. Many Hispanic groceries sell the pasilla shredded or ground. These reddish-brown chiles convey a heat range (amount of capsaicin) from a mild 10,000 to a popping 55,000 in the Scoville heat index and impart a rich, smoky flavor.

There are many different green chiles, but Anaheim or pasilla is a safe bet for a mild flavor. The real heat generators will be yellowish-green Jamaican hots or habanero chiles, and they make jalapeno seem mild, coming in at up to 200,000 on the Scoville scale. Substitute accordingly.

Regardless of what chiles you use, start with a little, let it cook for 20 minutes, then taste and adjust. If you use too much, too soon, it will sneak up on you.

Dominican Republic Invasion Mango Flan

A Layover On Hispaniola – When 300 gun-toting GIs got off a Jumbo Jet at the Dominican Republic's Puerto Plata airport, it wasn't really an invasion. Well, at least it wasn't an intentional invasion.

The GIs, the command staff for the general running America's peacekeeping mission in Haiti, were 129 miles away from the rest of soldiers invading in Port-au-Prince, Haiti, that September in 1994. Bad weather, mechanical problems and tactical concerns had diverted the chartered jet from Fort Bragg.

The handful of police and security guards patrolling the airport put down their weapons and stood aside as the troop swarmed into the sparkling new air terminal. The Americans followed a well-rehearsed

Above: A manager fills out paperwork beneath a mural of Jose Marti and Che Guevara inside a rum factory near Havana, Cuba, in November 2014. Photo by Kathy Best

military plan. From colonels to corporals, male and female, young and old, the drill was the same. Heavy combat boots quickly came off. A couch, a piece of carpet, a corner of the terminal was seized—any swath of terminal floor where they might not get stepped on. With weapons by their side and helmets for pillows, the general staff went to sleep.

What else might you expect from a flight where the attendant had instructed: "Ladies and gentlemen, please place your weapons under your seats with their barrels pointed toward the side of the aircraft."

This was the challenge: U.S. troops couldn't leave, and the food vendors couldn't get inside the terminal.

But baskets of fruit were supplied by the airlines, and it went well with the olive drab MREs. Renne Mittia, a vacationing chef from Santo Domingo, passed time waiting for her plane showing some of the troops how to peel and eat the jewel of the tropic fruit basket, the mango.

Here is the recipe for mango flan, her favorite dessert.

Ingredients for 8 servings

Water	½ cup
Turbinado (raw) sugar	1½ cups
Dark rum	4 T
Very ripe mango, pureed (roughly one and a half large mangoes)	3 cups
White sugar	5 T
Fresh ginger, minced	1 t
Lime zest, finely sliced	1 T
Orange juice	1 T
Lime juice	1 T
Eggs	6
Sweet cream or half-and-half	1 cup

First, glaze eight 8-oz ramekins or flan cups with sugar syrup. Heat water and raw sugar in a small pan over a low burner until the sugar melts. Add the rum. Slowly bring the mixture to a low boil for about 5 minutes or until the sugar darkens to a caramel color and it begins to thicken.

Divide into the eight ramekins with care. Tilt and swirl so the sides are coated with the glaze. Set aside.

Puree the mango in a blender at least one minute until smooth.

In a heavy pan, mix mango, white sugar, ginger, lime zest, and juice. Cook over a medium heat until a gentle boil, stirring 4 minutes.

Lightly beat the eggs and cream. When the mango mixture has cooled, mix in eggs and cream or half and half. Blend well.

Spoon into the sugared ramekins, tapping each on counter to level the flan mixture. Cover each ramekin tightly with foil, set in roasting pan and pour in about ½ inch of boiling water. Place in the oven preheated to 350 degrees for about 55 minutes or until a knife blade comes out clean.

Cool. Chill overnight or for at least 6 hours.

To remove, run knife blade around inside of each dish. Put a plate on top and invert. Flan should slide out in a few minutes.

Garnish with a thin slice of lime.

Florida Flamingo Grilled Shrimp

Flamingo is the southernmost point on mainland Florida. South of the Everglades. North of the Keys. Just an evening's speedboat ride from Cuba.

It is said that Flamingo and the numerous coves along the Bay of Florida are where Cuban patriots kept their boats and weapons ready to take their homeland back from the Communist dictator Fidel Castro.

We sat around a pile of burning driftwood and watched Papa Jose. He pointed due south and with great theatrics bellowed: "It's just 90 miles to where the devil lives. Just 90 miles to our home."

Jose talked of being a major in Alpha 66, the sometimes-CIA-funded invasion force of thousands, then hundreds, now tens, that practiced for decades to take back the homeland.

Roberto was not impressed, having heard every possible version of his father's tirade for years.

Gil, really Guillermo, age eight, was either mesmerized by the war stories or had the very unexpected grace to make believe his grandpa's tales captured him as intensely as the newest video game.

Old Cubans were probably really unhappy when Castro finally died. Part of it has to do with losing the enemy you know for one you don't. But more pain will come from losing someone you savored hating for decades.

The smell of the grilled shrimp brought back the women. It took just the slightest shake of Maria's head to end her husband's storytelling.

If the shrimp is to be cooked on wooden skewers, peel the shells off. If they are to be tossed on a fine-meshed grill, leave the shells on. Mix all the ingredients for the marinade well.

Some prefer hotter red chiles. I want to retain the taste of the shrimp so I use the mild green chile or Old Bay seasoning.

Above Left: Shrimp sizzle on a block of salt in one of Schneider's many Seattle kitchens. Photo by Andrew Schneider

Ingredients for 5-6 servings

Maggi or soy sauce	¼ cup
Dark rum	¼ cup
Dark brown sugar	2 T
Lime juice	2 T
Mild green chiles, chopped	1 T
(hotter chiles may be used but don't overwhelm the shrimp)	
Garlic, minced	4 cloves
Red onion, minced	1 cup
Fresh cilantro, chopped	1 T
Extra virgin olive oil	2 T
Cumin	1 t
Shrimp	2 lbs., extra large if possible

Mix all the ingredients for the marinade (everything but the shrimp) well.

Add the shrimp to the marinade for an hour, mixing frequently. If using wooden skewers, soak them well (15-30 minutes) to prevent burning.

Thread about 4 jumbo or 6 medium shrimp on two skewers, one through the heads of the shrimp and the other through the tails. The double skewers allow easy flipping of the shrimp. (Indoors, you could also cook them on a block of salt.)

Don't cook the shrimp until the rest of the meal is ready. Over a medium to hot fire, it only takes about two minutes on each. Brush with marinade before flipping.

When the shrimp are pink, they're ready to eat. Try to avoid overcooking, which can happen very quickly.

Garnish with slices of mango, lime, or both.

Hurricane Vegetable Paella. Photo by Keven McDermott

Florida Hurricane Vegetable Paella

To those working as rescuers after Hurricane Andrew slammed and leveled a good hunk of South Florida, fresh water was as important as food, and for many communities, especially the poorer ones, there was little of either.

This worried Barbara Mills. She was an unlikely looking Salvation Army disaster worker. Mid-20-something, dressed in brief denim shorts, long, black rubber swamp boots, and long red hair tucked under a white hard hat with "I work for God" scrawled on one side and a Harley emblem on the other, she stomped down the debris-strewn mud roads outside Homestead like she owned them.

It was eight sweltering days since the storm destroyed so many lives, and five since Mills and four other social workers from a graduate program in Pennsylvania raced south to help, she said.

She was checking out rumors from a sheriff's deputy that several camps of migrant workers had been overlooked or flat out ignored by the Red Cross and other flashier disaster aid groups.

She found them. At the end of the road, clustered under some tattered canvas tarps strung around some scrawny pine trees were about 40 or 50 people. The elderly, frustrated and weak. The children, frightened, wide-eyed and hungry. Whatever meat that had existed had spoiled. Nothing but sandwiches for days, and the peanut butter had run out. Mills sought out the oldest woman in the camp, and with the woman—someone's 87-year-old great-grandmother from Guatemala—in tow, the pair scoured the camp collecting whatever vegetables, roots, grain and spices were available.

She ordered the men to take sheet metal, which the storm had scattered all over the place, and fashion a very large, thin, wide pan, scrub it clean with sand and build a fire pit under a salvaged mattress spring to serve as a grill. Within two hours they had created a vegetable rice stew for 60.

I made a few modifications and call it Hurricane Vegetable Paella.

Ingredients for 12 servings

Red onion, cubed	1 large
Spanish onion, diced	1 large
Snow or snap peas	½ lb.
Asparagus, top half only	1 lb.
Celery, sliced ½" thick	3 stalks
Red pepper, cubed ½" thick	1.5
Green pepper, cubed ½" thick	1.5
Yellow squash, sliced ½" thick	1.5
Zucchini, sliced ½" thick	1.5
Plum or Roma tomatoes in ¼" slices	5
Old Bay Seasoning	1 T
Kosher salt	1 t
Black pepper	½ t
Olive oil, extra virgin, or butter	3 T
Garlic, shaved or minced	4 cloves
Turmeric	1 t
Cumin	½ t
Broth, vegetable, chicken, or seafood	4 cups
Rice, long grain	2 cups

Preheat oven to 400 degrees.

Cut the vegetables as instructed, keeping the Spanish onion in a separate bowl. Lay the rest of the vegetables on an oiled, foil-lined sheet pan. Sprinkle with half the garlic, turmeric, Old Bay, salt, and pepper. Drizzle with olive oil. Mix well and set aside.

In a medium saucepan, heat the diced Spanish onion in the olive oil. Add the cumin and the remaining half of the garlic, turmeric, salt, pepper, and Old Bay, stirring until onions soften.

Add broth and bring to a boil. Add the rice and stir well. Cover and reduce heat to a bare simmer. Cook without stirring until the water is absorbed and the rice is tender, about 20 minutes.

Remove from the heat and let sit, covered 10 minutes without stirring.

Meanwhile, place the pan with the sliced veggies and cubed red onion in the pre-heated oven; gently stir every 10 minutes until browned and tender. Remove from heat and set aside.

When the rice is finished, fluff with a fork, spread on a platter, cover with roasted vegetables, and serve.

Haiti Map Debat Patriot Stew

In Haiti, *map debat* means *shit happens*, and that phrase sums up much of life on the beleaguered island.

It was about 2 a.m. The roar of a huge Air Force cargo jet could still be heard as the word spread that the U.S. government had finally flown Baby Doc Duvalier, his family and chests of gold to France. Like fire roaring through dry timber, the word raced through Port-au-Prince. Within an hour the streets were alive with screams of joy and music.

Quickly, a mob swarmed over the iron gates of Baby Doc's mansion. While most searched for jewels and gold, six cooks from nearby hotels and restaurants headed for the dictator's overflowing freezers and pantries. Whatever was found was thrown into 20-gallon pots, seasoned and cooked over gas burners dragged into the street.

As the sun rose over a free Haiti for the first time in decades, four huge pots of food were loaded onto a truck and driven to a tiny church in the slums of Cite Soleil, where hundreds feasted on the dictator's food. They ate quickly, knowing that in Haiti, *map debat*.

This is a modification of the Patriot Stew served that morning in Haiti.

Left: Map Debat Patriot Stew. Photo by David McCumber

Ingredients for 12-15 servings

Olive oil, extra virgin	4 oz.
Chicken breasts or thighs, boned, cubed	4 lbs.
4 Italian sausages (about 1¼ pounds), cut 1" thick	
About ¾ lb of Chorizo sausage, preferably Spanish, cut ⅓" thick	
Tasso, in ½" cubes	½ lb.
Flour	2 T
Garlic, shaved	4 cloves
Pearl onions, peeled	2 cups small
Carrots, julienned	5 oz.
Mushrooms, white or shiitake, quartered	¾ lb.
Roma tomato, cut in ¼" slices	¾ lb.
Tomatoes, crushed	1 lb.
Red wine	½ cup
Dark rum	1 cup
Chicken stock	1½ quarts
Cumin, ground	½ t
Old Bay Seasoning	1½ t
White pepper	½ t
Kosher salt	1 t
Orange peel, candied	1½ oz.
Sweet red pepper, cut in ¼" slices,	1 cup
Green pepper, cut in ¼" slices	1¼ cups
Mango, cubed	2⅛ cups
Shrimp, shelled	25 large

In a large heavy pan, over medium flame, heat the olive oil; add the chicken and cook until lightly browned, about 4 minutes. Add pearl onions, carrots, mushrooms and cook, stirring, another couple of minutes until partially browned, finishing with the garlic.

Add the sausage, chorizo and Tasso and cook for 3 minutes; add flour and stir well. Add Roma tomatoes, crushed tomatoes, wine, rum, chicken stock, and seasonings. Bring to boil, lower heat, cover, and simmer for 30 minutes.

Check seasonings; add red and green pepper and mango, stir gently, and cook covered for 8 minutes.

Add shelled shrimp, cook for 2 minutes. Stir well but gently.

Serve over white or yellow rice.

Haiti Armando's Cuban Pork

The GIs in Haiti ate MREs only until they could find real food. Armando ate the best food the Haitian hotels were offering—until he could find something better. As with everything Armando did, this is wonderful. It does things to pork that may be illegal. The aroma alone, as it cooks, is almost worth the effort.

Ingredients for 8 servings

Olive oil, extra virgin	1 T
Cumin seeds, crushed	2 t
Green peppercorn, crushed	1 t
Garlic, slivered	6 cloves
Adobo (bitter orange) or salt	1 t
Maggi	2 T
Vermouth, white	½ cup
Limes, pulp only	2 large
Orange juice, fresh	⅔ cup
Boneless pork roast, tied	4 lbs.
Orange zest	1 T

In a small saucepan, heat the olive oil with the cumin, green peppercorn, garlic, Adobo or salt, and Maggi.

Stir while bringing to a boil; add vermouth and immediately lower heat. Simmer for two minutes.

When cool, add lime pulp, orange juice and orange zest.

Put pork roast in a sealed container or plastic bag, add marinade, and coat well. Refrigerate, occasionally turning meat, for at least 3 hours; overnight is better.

Cook at 325 degrees for about 2 hours and 15 minutes (for medium) or until desired doneness. Baste with marinade throughout.

Let rest 15 minutes, then slice and serve with lack beans, rice or plantains to make Armando happy.

THE CHAPARE, Bolivia–As if the oppressive jungle heat didn't make them wet enough, DEA Snowcap teams must cross dozens of rivers and streams as they hunt for drug labs during Operation Ghose Zone.
Photo by Andrew Schneider/Scripps Howard News Service

II

Latin America

1989-1993

Scripps Howard News Service

THE CHAPARE, Bolivia—Brian Donaldson, an ex-special forces medic from Fairfax, Va., is part of the DEA Snowcap team assigned to Operation Ghost Zone that is tracking 22 Bolivian drug organizations, from the chemical couriers trudging in the jungle mud to the money-laundering banker in their corporate offices. Photo by Andrew Schneider/Scripps Howard News Service

Latin America

In an infamous speech on Sept. 5, 1989, President George H.W. Bush held up an evidence bag of crack cocaine on national television and said he was going to wage war on drugs, which he called the "greatest domestic threat facing our nation today."

According to The *Washington Post*, Bush "drew a direct connection between crime in the inner city and cocaine production in Columbia and South America ... Wherever traffickers operated, they could expect to be met by American power." The Post reported that the Pentagon's counternarcotics budget increased "by over 100,000 percent" between 1982 and the end of Bush's presidency.

That kind of spending increase was catnip for investigative reporters. So Andy and fellow Scripps Howard Washington Bureau reporter Peter Copeland headed to South America to see for themselves how the money was being spent—and if the war was being won.

Here's what they found, from their project called The Drug Warriors: "More than 20 federal agencies have staked out territory in the drug war. Each has its own battle plan. Each has its own war chest filled by Congress. Each has its own troops in Latin America. It's the biggest U.S. operation ever in Latin America. There's just one missing element. This war has no general in charge, either in Washington or in Latin America ... The coordination of operations among U.S. agencies, when there is any, is liked by one drug warrior to a 'pickup' softball team."

To reach those conclusions, Andy and Peter traveled throughout Columbia, Ecuador, Peru, and Bolivia, sometimes defying death on narrow roads through the Andes. Andy focused on interviewing Americans in the field and on the people in the small mountain and seaside towns where the drug warriors operated.

In any story he covered, Andy was all in. Yet he always found time to explore the local food culture.

Cochabamba, Bolivia, was a resort town. And judging from the recipes he brought home, a foodie town, too. Preparations for steak with ginger marinade, yam pancakes and a sauce of rosemary, beef broth and wine all came from there. Quito, Ecuador, provided a recipe for tropical fruit pork. And Chapare, Bolivia, inspired the DEA's chicken plus scallops or prawns.

While he loved cooking main dishes, soup was Andy's true passion. And he found several in Latin America. A black bean soup with chorizo, cloves, brown sugar and dark rum. A sopa de Lima with chicken breasts, limes, grape tomatoes, onion and cilantro. A pork, mushroom and cilantro soup from the shores of Lake Titicaca, which sits at 12,508 feet above sea level and separates Bolivia and Peru. And a tarragon and fennel soup that Helena McDonald Sanchez of Colon, Panama, told Andy was a family favorite. Her grandmother, she told him when they met in a market in Colon, called it Panamanian penicillin and "insisted it fought jungle bacteria and infections better than anything from a pharmacy."

His favorite, however, came from a chance encounter when heavy rains forced the Ecuadorian and American drug warriors he was traveling with to beach their boats along the Amazon River near Coca, Ecuador. Carmelita Bushe, who lived in the village, provided food for the unexpected guests, including a monkey head served up to the guest at the head of the table. Andy, relieved he wasn't sitting there, stuck to the soup—an Amazonian version of gazpacho. Ms. Bushe made it with vegetables smoked over lemon wood, chiles and corn.

—Kathy Best

Latin America

Bolivia
Cochabamba Steak With Ginger Marinade

Ecuador
Ecuadorian Citrus Shrimp Soup
Rio Coca Amazonian Gazpacho

Panama
Tarragon and Fennel Soup

Bolivia — Cochabamba Steak With Ginger Marinade

One of the world's spookiest over-the-mountain passages has to be the five-hour run to this Bolivian resort city from the Chapare Jungle.

Just imagine nightmare fodder for the worst B-movie: battered old trucks overloaded with enormous mahogany logs, brakes spewing dark smoke, barrelling down the one-lane mud road along a winding path that has no guardrails. Rusted hulks of buses, trucks and burnt-out cars littering the jungle floor hundreds of feet below.

A ramshackle combination chapel, auto repair stop and cafe at the top of the pass gets a lot of visitors.

You just know you're going to die, but eventually most travelers make it to Cochabamba.

This ginger steak is a spin-off of a recipe that a DEA agent made for us before we started over the mountain. It's a hell of a last meal.

Ingredients for 1-2 servings

Ginger root, sliced into thin sticks	1 small
Peanut or corn oil	2 T
Sirloin steak	1 lb
Marinade	
Tequila	¼ cup
Mojo Criollo (Spanish citrus BBQ sauce)	1 T
Maggi sauce	1 T
Worcestershire sauce	1 T
Garlic, minced	1 T
Salt, fine	¼ t
Black pepper, fine	¼ t
Dry red wine	¾ cup

Mix the marinade and pour over the steak in a plastic bag.

Seal, then place in a bowl in the refrigerator for 2 to 3 hours. Remove steak, reserving marinade, and warm to room temperature before cooking.

Fry ginger in peanut or corn oil until browned. Season and keep warm.

Grill beef over hot fire for 4½ minutes on each side for a 1½" thick steak.

Remove steak from the fire and let it rest for 10 minutes. Meanwhile, add ¾ cup dry red wine to the reserved marinade and, in a small saucepan, slow boil until reduced by two-thirds. Remove from heat, cut the fried ginger sticks in half, and mix into sauce. Serve over steak.

Ecuador — Ecuadorian Citrus Shrimp Soup

The park had the look of the Smithsonian Museum's annual folk festival. Native people in tents and huts cooked traditional meals over wood fires in a sprawling green in the shadow of the Capitol.

This time, in the summer of 1992, the Capitol buildings were in Quito, Ecuador, and those cooking in the park were 2,000 Indians of 11 different indigenous groups. Many marched for 20 days to get to the Capitol, some traveling 300 miles deep in the Amazon region, to force legislators to protect their lands from multinational oil, mining, and logging companies stripping the jungle. A prime target for some was to halt the plans of a Texas chemical company to cut a highway through the environmentally sensitive jungle. The Dallas company, according to the protest signs, produced the lethal Agent Orange used in Vietnam.

Ethnic identity is paramount to these groups, and it was the first time anyone could recall a gathering of tribes from more than 100 villages. The participants, comfortable with the humid, tropical weather of the jungle, were unaccustomed to the chill of Quito and to the efforts by police to get many to wear clothing that concealed more than did their jungle garb.

As the protest lingered from days into weeks, food became a problem. The supplies they brought had just about run out, and supporters were buying food from local markets, many strange to those Indians from remote villages. All villages use corn and the potato-like yucca in various ways. Citrus, bananas, plantains are staples for some. For those from villages on or near the coast, seafood is heavily used.

A month into the protest, many different groups were pooling their food and creating new recipes. One such collusion was among the Quichua and Shiwiar tribes from the central Amazon region and Guayaquilenlos, from the Bay of Guayaquil. This is an adaptation of what they threw into their communal soup pot.

Ingredients for 6 servings

Corn oil	3 T
Kosher salt	1 t
White pepper	¼ t
Shrimp, with shells	1 lb.
Garlic, roasted or fried until soft	6 cloves
Shallots or sweet onion, chopped fine	½ cup
Yucca, diced small	1 cup
Corn, cut off cobs	2 ears
Orange zest	4 T
Lemon zest	2 T
Fish (or chicken) stock	6 cups
Paprika	½ t
Cumin, ground	¼ t
Hot sauce	to taste
Cilantro, chopped fine,	2 T

Heat the oil in a heavy pot or Dutch oven over moderate heat. Add half the salt and pepper and the shrimp still in shells. Cook for about 2 minutes on each side. Remove shrimp from pot and set aside until cool.

When shrimp are cool, remove shells and heads and place in a cheesecloth bag. Either sauté whole garlic cloves until soft or roast cloves wrapped in foil with a teaspoon of olive oil at 400 degrees for 40 minutes

Mash the garlic with a fork and add with shallots or onion, yucca, and corn to a Dutch oven. Stir for about 2 minutes or until lightly browned. Add orange and lemon zest; stir and add the fish or chicken stock and the bag of shrimp shells. Bring to a boil, lower heat, and simmer for 30 minutes.

Add paprika, cumin, hot sauce, and remaining salt and pepper. Stir.

Add the peeled shrimp and simmer for 2 minutes.

Remove bag of shrimp shells, adjust seasonings, garnish with cilantro, and serve.

Ecuador Rio Coca Amazonian Gazpacho

It was an unusual party, even by the standards accepted along the Amazon. Two dozen soggy drug warriors—Ecuadorians and Americans—trying to avoid the surging debris on the rapidly rain-swelling river, forced their high-powered boats up onto the beach near a village of good guys, or at least neutrals, in the drug war.

Carmelita Bushe, the surprised hostess who lives near Coca, Ecuador, where the Napo River cuts through the rainforests of El Oriente, looked like a thinner version of Bloody Mary from *South Pacific*, even down to teeth stained a pale red. She appeared a bit threatening, but she could cook. Within two hours of our unexpected arrival she and her "kitchen crew" hauled out banana leaf platters overflowing with fish, some kind of pork, scrawny fowl of some unknown origin and of course, the ever-popular monkey head. Just as some Arab tribes insist the honored guest be served the sheep's eyes, our guide from the Ecuadorian drug police whispered to me that gracious dining Amazon–style offers up the monkey to the person sitting at the head of the table. Fortunately, it was not me.

Of the varied, colorful and fragrant foods she offered up, her "cold vegetable soup" seemed the safest. This is an adaptation of Ms. Bushe's recipe. She smoked most of the vegetables over lemon wood, but, with the exception of the chiles and the corn, this version uses uncooked vegetables.

Some think that the key to this recipe is uniformity in the sizes of the veggie pieces. If you want it smoother, use an in-pot blender at a low to medium speed and blend for 15 or 20 seconds at most. Please don't overdo it and make it mushy. When possible, I prepare this the day or night before, always at least several hours before serving, so the flavors will blend.

Ingredients for 20 servings

Yellow River, green or banana pickled chiles, charred	6
Red, green, yellow sweet peppers, chopped in small pieces	6 large
Corn on cob, grilled, smoked or boiled	3
Tomato or V-8 juice	4 quarts
Olive oil, extra virgin	½ cup
Maggi sauce	3 T
Vinegar, red wine, shallot or citrus	½ cup
Adobo (sea salt, onion & garlic powder)	2 ½ t
Garlic, minced	4 cloves
Tomatoes, plum, chopped small pieces	2¼ lbs.
Onion, red, chopped fine	1¼ cup
Onions, green or scallion, white sliced fine	1 cup
Carrots, minced	2 large
Celery, sliced thin	3 stalks
Cucumber, peeled, seeded, chopped	3 large
Limes, zested and juiced	2
Cilantro leaves, chopped coarse	1 cup
Chipotle, ground	½ t
Salt, pepper, fire oil or hot sauce as needed	
Lime, sliced thin	1

Optional

Liquid smoke	½ t

Over a stove burner or under a broiler, char the chiles until the skin is blackened in spots. Put in a paper or plastic bag and let sit for 5 minutes. When cool enough to touch, use the edge of a knife to scrape skin off. Cut chili length wise, rinse out the seed (don't touch your eyes) and chop into small pieces. Set aside. If you can't char the peppers, it is okay to serve cold, but you must wash the seeds out and dice very small.

Cook corn by method of choice. Let cool and remove kernels from cob. Set aside.

Add the chilled V-8 or tomato juice to a large soup pot plus olive oil, Maggi, vinegar, and adobo. Add minced garlic, corn, chiles, peppers, diced tomatoes, and red and green onions.

Cut the carrots and celery and add. You don't have to peel the cucumbers but, unless using seedless English cukes, cut them in half lengthwise and use a teaspoon to scrape out the seeds. Chop small and add to the pot.

Zest the lime onto a paper towel and add to the pot. Cut the limes in half and squeeze juice into the pot. Slice one lime very thin to use as garnish when served. Bunch the cilantro and chop finely with a knife, avoiding the end stems, Add. Stir.

Add powdered chipotle, salt and pepper, stir, taste, adding more Maggi if needed plus liquid smoke and hot sauce if desired.

Garnish with thin lime slices or a few celery or cilantro leaves and serve well chilled.

Panama Tarragon and Fennel Soup

I modified this from a recipe by Helena McDonald Sanchez in Colon, Panama.

Helena said this was a family favorite. Her grandmother called it Panamanian penicillin and insisted it fought jungle bacteria and infections better than anything from a pharmacy. It can be served hot or chilled.

Ingredients for 4 servings

Olive oil	2 T
Shallots, minced	3 T
Garlic, minced	1 T
Fennel, fresh, chopped fine	1 bulb
Chicken or veggie stock	6 cups
Zucchini, sliced thin	2 cups
Tarragon, fresh, finely minced	1 T
Lemon juice	2 T
Lemon zest	2 t
Sea salt	½ t
White pepper	¼ t
Maggi or dark soy sauce	1 t
Grape tomatoes, halved	1 cup

In a large pot, heat olive oil over medium heat. Add shallots, garlic, and fennel. Cook, stirring, until fennel is soft.

Add stock.

Add zucchini, tarragon, lemon juice and zest.

Add seasonings and Maggi or dark soy sauce.

Bring to a boil, quickly lower to a simmer, and cover for 10 minutes.

Add grape tomatoes and simmer for another 10 minutes. Check and adjust spices. Serve with either a sprig of dill or some chopped fennel fronds.

III

The American South

1963-1992

*Schneider stirs the roux in his kitchen on the Chesapeake Bay in 2007.
Photo by Paul Kitagaki Jr.*

The American South

Conflict and chaos typically lured Andy to the South. Assaults on civil rights marchers. Hurricanes. Rotting railroad bridges. Devastating floods.

But at least he could eat well and use his reporter's notebook to capture techniques, ingredients and flavors to bring home. As one of those cardboard pads noted: "Some of the best eating comes after the hurricane has passed."

Even in the absence of storms, Andy was intrigued by how people in the South coped with their environment, from the curing of country ham to the brining of birds. "Sometimes a hunter would get a great bird a couple of days before it was going to be cooked and it became a race between the meat turning bad and getting cooked. Cooks from Little Tybee Island near Savannah, Georgia, to Currituck, North Carolina, just south of the Great Dismal Swamp, came up with the idea of soaking the bird—whatever species—in a clean barrel of saltwater fresh from the Atlantic," he wrote.

Andy would mine the memories of roadhouse cooks in Alabama and Louisiana in search of authentic red-eye gravy recipes. He'd talk meat there with men whose hands were stained from rubbing spices and herbs onto briskets, shoulders and butts. He loved the blending of cuisines—African, French, Spanish—that produced dishes like shrimp and grits.

I was never a fan of hot weather, so Andy lured me to Charleston with the promise that its cooks served some of the best food in America. I ended up eating shrimp and grits every day for a week. It became our go-to meal for New Year's Eve as we bounced from coast to coast, both of which, thankfully, have shrimpers.

—Kathy Best

The American South

Alabama
Moses' Porkin' Heaven Rub

Georgia
Gandy Dancer Dirty Rice

Louisiana
Everyman's Gumbo

North Carolina
Preacher's Red-Eye Gravy

South Carolina
And God Said "Country Ham"
Blindman's Grits and Ham
Shrimp and Grits

Alabama Moses' Porkin' Heaven Rub

This magic mixture is from Moses Jones, who was 99 years old when he shared this fantastic rub with me at his grandson's boiled peanut stand outside Dothan, Alabama. Most people, he says—"especially white Yankees"—have no idea of what cookin' over a fire is all about. "If it's too hot to lay your hand on the top of the smoker, you're not smoking, you're roastin'," Moses told me, pointing to his leathery hard palm.

The secret to this, or any other great seasoning for smoked or roasted meat, is to "rub it in hard and deep, like you're making love to that hunk of pig."

This recipe is my adaptation.

Ingredients for 6 servings

Turbinado or raw cane sugar	2 T
Maple sugar or crystals	2 T
Lemon-pepper blend	2 T
Cumin, ground	1 t
Mustard powder	1 T
Mustard seed	1 t
Paprika, Hungarian sweet	1 T
Kosher salt	1 T
Pasilla or chipotle chiles, powdered	½ t
Pork butt or baby back ribs	5 lbs.

Mix all the spices together.

Rinse the meat and pat dry well.

Coat heavily with mixture and rub in well on all sides.

Wrap seasoned meat in foil or seal in a plastic bag.

Keep overnight, if possible, or at least for four hours.

Smoke slowly, at about 250 degrees, for about one to two hours a pound, depending on the thickness of the meat.

"Best to do over some fine fruity wood," Moses says.

Georgia Gandy Dancer Dirty Rice

Old railroaders grumbled a lot, but they actually took pride in the food they were fed at the rail camps. Living in movable bunkhouses for weeks on end, they repaired and laid steel rails throughout the Southeastern United States.

The track workers used large sledgehammers to set the spikes and steel pry bars to move the ties. It wasn't surprising that the men were tagged nationwide as Gandy Dancers, so the unverified story goes, considering that a company named Gandy made railyard tools.

Like soldiers, railroad crews traveled on their stomachs, and adequate grub was one of the few perks of back-breaking jobs. The railroads often supplied the food or gave the crews money to buy it from local farmers. However, the corporations didn't supply the cooks, and often the most readily available culinary wizards were the very same hobos they'd been chasing off their trains all day.

A truce was called at dinnertime and both sides benefitted. This recipe came from a fellow who identified himself as Chancy of Savannah, who told me he'd ridden the Seaboard Coastline Railroad between Miami and South Carolina for three decades. He proudly showed me his banjo, a small iron skillet that most hobos treasured.

Ingredients for 10 servings

Garlic cloves, minced	5
Chicken gizzards	1 lb.
Rice, long grain	3 cups
Peanut or olive oil	3 T
Chicken liver, trimmed	1 lb.
Pork, coarse chili cut	1 lb.
Celery, sliced ¼" thick	3 stalks
Chicken stock	6 cups
Cilantro, chopped	½ cup
Cumin, ground	½ t
Black pepper, coarse	½ t
Old Bay seasoning	½ t
Kosher salt	½ t
Mustard powder, dry	1 t
Celery seed	2 t
Green onion, roughly chopped	¾ cups
Red pepper, sliced	1 ¼ cups

In a saucepan, cover gizzards with water and bring to boil. Add garlic and simmer for 45 minutes over low heat. Set aside, cool, and chop finely. Reserve liquid as part of rice-cooking stock.

In a lidded saucepan, bring 6 cups stock to boil. Add rice, return to a boil, cut heat, and simmer for 20 minutes.

In a heavy skillet, heat oil. Brown liver for two minutes. Remove, cool, and chop finely. Add pork, celery and red pepper and cook for 4 minutes.

Add chopped gizzards and seasonings. Cook over medium heat for 10 minutes.

Add chopped liver and cook for 1 minute, stirring.

Add meat mixture to cooked rice, finishing with green onions.

Serve hot.

Louisiana Everyman's Gumbo

The heart of this gumbo came from an Acadian who had moved back to Canada. But in August 1992, just after Hurricane Andrew bounced off Florida and slammed into Central Louisiana, he rushed back to his family home in Atchafalaya to help his old friends living in the Delta.

Those with food or live catches tossed whatever vegetables, meat, seafood and spices they had left after the storm into a well-scrubbed, half-55-gallon drum and made rice in the other half of the steam-cleaned drum. It may be the first time that roux—the wonderful Cajun thickening agent—was ever blended in the bottom of a steel drum. Knowing those fine people, it probably wasn't.

This recipe is my modification of that great gumbo, pulled from the cuisine of Africa, Spain and France. It seemed to feed everyone who showed up that soggy summer week.

Yes, for you purists, I know his recipe does not use okra, but it's as it was made by people who grew up with gumbo.

Many, including me, prefer to cook shrimp with heads on. It adds lots of flavor.

Some don't think using whole crawfish is worth the effort and either use picked crawfish meat or add more crab.

Ingredients for 12 servings as a main, 20 as a soup

Roux

Bacon fat, duck fat, lard, butter, or oil	1½ cups
All-purpose flour	1½ cups
Smoked bacon	8 slices

Gumbo

Shrimp, large or jumbo, shelled	3 lb.
Blue crab, picked clean	1½ lb.
Crawfish tails shelled, cleaned	1½ lb.
Celery cut in ½" pieces	3 stalks
Green pepper, cut in ½" pieces	1½ cup
Onions, cut in ½" pieces	2 cups
Red pepper, cut in ½" pieces	1½ cup
Garlic, minced	8 cloves
Andouille or other spicy smoked sausage, cut ¼" thick	1 lb.
Tasso (Cajun smoked pork) in chunks	1 lb.
Chicken, boned in bite-sized pieces	2 lbs.
Shrimp, fish, or chicken stock	10 cups
Green onions cut in ½" pieces	10
Cooked rice	12 cups
Bay leaves	2
Thyme	2 T
Old Bay seafood seasoning	2 T

Optional

Okra, sliced ¼" thick	1½ lb

Above left: Fennel, country ham, sausage, crab legs, shrimp and veggies await the pot. Photo by Andrew Schneider

Clean the shrimp, crab and crawfish and set aside, reserving shells for stock.

Make stock. If using shrimp or seafood shells or bones, strain carefully and set aside. If using stock from store, consider blend of fish and chicken.

Cut vegetables and garlic and set aside.

Into a heavy, 12-quart stockpot or enameled Dutch oven, make roux to a medium brown as described below. Fat from eight pieces of cooked bacon and duck fat is my favorite base.

When roux is ready, quickly add vegetables and garlic. Stir well over medium heat for five minutes or until soft. Add sausage and tasso and cook for another five minutes, stirring well.

Add chicken and cook for five minutes.

Slowly add in stock and add bay leaves, thyme and Old Bay. Bring to a boil, and lower to simmer. Cook for 60 minutes, stirring well.

Add crawfish and okra, if using, and simmer for 15 minutes.

Add shrimp and crab meat for final 5 minutes. Stir, remove pot from heat, and let it sit for at least 10 minutes.

Garnish with chopped green onion and serve over rice as a main dish, or just about a ½ cup in a bowl for soup.

Making your roux:

Here is where you make or break almost every Cajun dish you create.

A roux is a one-to-one mixture of flour to equal amount butter, duck fat, lard, bacon fat or olive oil. Put your oil over medium heat in the bottom of a heavy pot that will hold the gumbo. Add about one-half of the flour to the heated oil or butter, stirring well with a wooden spoon or flat-edged wooden spatula for at least 30 seconds. When well mixed, slowly add another portion of flour and keep it up until all the flour is in the pan. You must stir the roux constantly, never leaving the pot, not to pee, yell at the dogs or answer the door, until the roux is a dark, rich mahogany or chocolate in color. Anticipate a wonderful aroma when the roux is nearly just perfect.

The lower the heat, the slower the cooking, the better it will be. You could be cooking for about 30 minutes depending on the heat. It seems to go faster with zydeco playing in the background.

North Carolina Preacher's Red-Eye Gravy

This could also be called Peace-keeper Gravy because the Methodist minister who formulated this magic mixture brought peace to a beautiful North Carolina valley where country ham and gravy are believed as sacred as a sunrise. The key, according to the reverend, "is a skillet that knows its mission," which translates to a heavy-bottomed pan. For old time's sake, I like an iron skillet.

Ingredients for 3 servings

Peanut oil	2 t
Country ham or tasso, slivered	⅓ cup
Shallots, minced	3 T
Coffee, strong, black	½ cup
Butter, sweet	3 T
Flour	⅓ cup
Chicken stock	3 cups
Brown sugar	½ t
Mustard	½ t
Salt and pepper	

Whatever skillet you use, heat the peanut oil on medium high, add the country ham, then stir well until the ham and pan bottom are both a dark golden brown.

Lower the heat to medium, add the shallots, stir for another minute or two until browned (not burnt), then add the coffee and a pea-sized piece of butter. Cook down until all the coffee is gone

Lower heat. Add the rest of the butter and slowly blend in the flour, stirring constantly until you get a "walnut-colored" roux. Be careful. The distance between a nutty-flavored roux and a charred useless mess can be just a matter of seconds.

Add half the stock, brown sugar, and mustard. Then increase the heat and stir well until the mixture thickens.

Lower heat and add remainder of stock, stirring well for another 10 to 20 minutes until it reduces to the consistency you're looking for.

Add salt, pepper, or hot sauce as needed. Some true believers also add a spot of whisky or a bit more mustard.

Serve warm.

South Carolina And God Said "Country Ham"

Old Southern preachers used to say that when something is deformed, ugly or out of place, but still brings joy and bliss, you know it has been touched by the hand of God. Many of those crowded into the stifling canvas tent in Spartanburg, South Carolina, knew the traveling preacher had to be talking about the mold-covered, green-tainted, misshapen country hams that hung from the spikes in the ceiling of their barns.

Today, in a world of health inspectors blessing shrink-wrapped, identically sized, color-enhanced, standardized food, the true country ham remains a sacred, vanishing culinary icon.

In Colonial days, salt curing was the answer to the lack of refrigeration, the only real way to ensure that meat could be kept until needed.

This recipe begins with locating and buying an authentic, salt-cured, air-dried country, and not one of the 30-day, commercial knockoffs being cranked out as the real thing. Depending to whom you're serving this blessed dish, it can take as long as three days to get it to the table. For those who grew up eating these revered hunks of meat, soaking the ham for at least a full night and day is a must. To those whose deprived upbringing did not expose them to what is really good, the salt should be calmed down by bathing the ham in frequently changed water for as long as three days. If you're worried about it still being too salty, find someone else to serve it to.

For the snobs who turn their noses up at the crudeness of a country ham, remind them that the fine Italian prosciutto embraced by the beautiful people at many dollars a pound is produced almost the same way.

To get started, run the ham under warm water and, with a stiff, clean brush, scrub off as much of the mold and seasonings as you can. Cover the ham with clean water and change every 12 hours.

The washing is about the only step upon which Deep South cooks agree. Everything else done to the meat changes not only from state to state, but often from farm to farm.

This recipe follows most of the steps used by my father to cook these hams as we were growing up in Florida. But in the spirit of full disclosure, I've got to tell you that dad came from Budapest, which is not exactly known for its Southern cuisine.

Above left: And God Said "Country Ham" Photo by Lore Postman

Ingredients for 30 servings

Real country ham	18 lbs.
Coca-Cola	1 cup
Southern beer or ale	1 cup
Cuban or dark rum	1 cup
Yellow mustard seed	1 T
Dark brown sugar	2 T

For glaze

Dark brown sugar	⅓ cup
Dijon mustard	3 T
Cloves, ground	½ t
Cinnamon, ground	½ t
Orange juice	2 T
Cuban or dark rum	2 T

After soaking the ham, preheat the oven to 500 degrees.

Place the ham, fat side up, in a large, covered roaster and add Coca-Cola, southern beer or ale, Cuban or dark rum, mustard seeds, dark brown sugar, and liquid to cover the ham. Cover or seal with foil.

Bake for 15 minutes, then lower the temperature to 325 degrees and cook for another 90 minutes. You want the ham to cook at a light simmer (no big bubbles).

Flip ham and cook for another 2 hours or until internal temperature reaches 165 degrees.

Remove the pan from the oven and let the ham cool in liquid.

When cooled, gash the skin and insert your hand to remove the skin and fat from the meat. Trim as much fat as you must but do leave at least a little.

Combine the seasonings into a paste and rub well into the ham. Bake at 350 degrees for 30 minutes or until the glaze has browned.

Remove from heat and let cool completely.

To serve: use a very sharp knife and slice ham paper thin, ⅛ inch or less. Serve with a wonderful Red Eye gravy (see Preacher's Red Eye Gravy).

Freeze bits and pieces for seasoning vegetables, pasta, eggs, and a dozen other dishes. The bones present a great head start on an outstanding pea soup.

South Carolina **Blind Man's Grits and Ham**

Frank Williams insists he's a better cook because he's blind.

"I pay a lot more attention to how food feels and smells than do my friends who can see what they're doing," says the 76-year-old former Army cook, who lost his vision during the first week of the Korean War.

"You develop a fine touch and that's surely what you need to do grits right," he says. "It's God's work."

Somehow, even without sight, he can tell white grits from yellow. He digs his hands into the two grain sacks stacked atop a 40-pound bag of rice.

"This is what you want for breakfast. Coarse, almost chunky," he says, running the yellow grain through his fingers. "The white stuff's okay if you want to show off with some gravy."

He caresses a hunk of country ham, sniffs it, gently lays it on a cutting board and slices it into strips about ¼ inch wide and an inch or less long. Then he sautés them over medium heat for about two minutes in a heavy pan.

To that, he adds onions. Sweet onions are best, he says. He prefers Vidalia, but Walla Walla, Maui or even a fresh Spanish onion will also do. He peels the onion, slices it about ¼ inch thick and dices it into chunks which are added to the cooking ham. If needed, he adds a bit of bacon fat or pure butter. And stirs.

He lowers the heat and cooks for about 8 minutes or until onions are golden, not browned. He stirs well.

Meanwhile, into a large, heavy saucepan, he brings the chicken stock to a boil and adds grits, stirring well.

He lowers heat under grits to a light simmer and cooks for 20-30 minutes. When cooked, he adds butter, salt and pepper and the ham and onion mixture.

If you prefer, they can be served separately.

Ingredients for 4 servings

Country ham	½ cup
Onion	⅓ cup
Chicken broth, rich	6 cups
Yellow grits, coarse	2 cups
Butter, sweet	5 T
Pepper & salt	

Above left: Blind Man's Ham and Grits. Photo by Lore Postman

South Carolina Shrimp and Grits (Or call it polenta)

This globe of ours is infested with food snobs, and the theory that "it's all in the name" is proven every day. People who know no better would rather starve before sitting down to a serving of grits. Yet they'll go to an expensive Italian restaurant and shell out top dollar for a bowl of polenta, adorned with anything.

Get over it. Grits and polenta are identical. Both come from corn meal, either white or yellow, either fine or coarse, and both are the foundation for some wonderful food. In the southeast corner of this country, grits are often blessed with a crowning of a flavorful blending of shrimp, tasso and side pork. Tasso is a wonderfully seasoned, lean, Cajun ham and side pork is like thick bacon.

For this recipe, if you can't get tomatoes in season, high-quality canned tomatoes are a better choice than the cardboard offered up as fresh in the fall and winter. If you can't get Tabasco with chipotle, add a couple of drops of liquid smoke, and it will come close to the flavor.

I adapted this recipe from Seabrook Island after Hurricane Hugo.

Ingredients for 4 servings

Water	2-3 cups
Chicken broth	2 cups
Grits, yellow	1 cup
Butter	2½ T
Cheddar cheese, sharp	2 oz.

Shrimp and tasso topping

Side pork (or bacon), sliced ¼" thick	⅛ lb.
Scallions sliced ⅓" thick, green and white	½ cup
Mushrooms, shiitake, sliced ¼" thick	½ cup
Garlic, minced	1½ cloves
Red pepper, diced small	2 T
Tasso sliced ¼" thick	¼ lb.
Oregano, dried	1½ t
Basil, dried	¼ t
Tomato, diced	½ cup
Shrimp, shelled	20 large
Heavy cream	½ cup
Kosher salt	½ t
Pepper, black	¼ t
Tabasco sauce with chipotle pepper	⅓ t
Worcestershire Sauce or Maggi	to taste

In a heavy saucepan, bring water and chicken broth to a boil. Add salt and pepper.

Add grits, stir, lower heat to a simmer.

Cook, stirring regularly, until water is absorbed (about 15 to 20 minutes), adding third cup of water if needed to give grits desired tooth.

Remove from heat, stir in butter and cheese, and set aside.

Shrimp and tasso topping

In a heavy skillet, slowly cook side pork or bacon until crisp. Set aside, reserving fat.

To the fat, add the scallions, mushroom, garlic, red pepper, tasso and sauté until soft. Do not overcook.

Add herbs and other seasonings and stir.

Add tomatoes and cook until soft

Add shrimp and sauté 45 seconds to 2 minutes until pink, depending on size of shrimp. Remove and set aside. If the topping mixture is too dry, add a bit of chicken broth.

Add heavy cream and stir over medium heat until blended.

Return shrimp and stir. Check seasonings, perhaps adding Tabasco, Worcestershire, or Maggi.

Stir gently, spoon over grits, and serve.

IV

Chesapeake Country and The Capital

1964-1995

Schneider and Best carefully load Maryland blue crabs into the pot in their kitchen on the Chesapeake Bay. Photo by Andrew Cutraro

Chesapeake Country

If Andy had a homebase, it would be the greater Washington area. He lived there during three different periods of his life. It's where his children, Patrick and Kelly, were born. It's where he made the transition from photographer to reporter. And it's where we met.

His first print job after getting out of the Army and back from Vietnam was with the *Montgomery County Sentinel*, a scrappy suburban newspaper that was a training ground for some of the best journalists in the business: Bob Woodward of *The Washington Post*, Knight Kiplinger of the Kiplinger financial media company, Robert Pear of *The New York Times*, to name a few. Roger B. Farquhar, the editor, was a gifted mentor and a Quaker with a temper. He threw a typewriter at Andy that sailed out a window, nearly hitting a judge, when Andy announced he wanted to write. Farquhar later wrote a letter apologizing after Andy won his first Pulitzer and was the inspiration for "A Great Teacher's Chesapeake Fish Stew" recipe.

Andy returned to Washington a second time after the *Pittsburgh Press* folded, going to work as the assistant managing editor for investigations in the Scripps Howard Washington Bureau, traveling the country and the world working on projects. When he was home, his house on Capitol Hill was a destination for friends and sources interested in good food and engaging conversation.

His third return to the region was to work at *The Baltimore Sun* as an investigative reporter for two years.

While Washington then had respectable cuisine on offer, it was the flavors on the Chesapeake that drew Andy—and none more than the blue crab.

One of our first dates was at Cantler's Riverside Inn outside Annapolis, a crab house where brown paper is laid on the table and steaming hot crabs are dumped in a pile along with mallets, knives and rolls of paper towels. We ate crabs whenever we could: at the home of dear friends in Fairhaven, at feasts on Andy's Constitution Avenue patio, at crab shacks in Maryland and Virginia and at the old Obrycki's restaurant in Fells Point, Baltimore. The latter's pepper-based crab seasoning was interesting but, in the end, didn't quite match up to Old Bay.

In Andy's kitchen, Old Bay and Wye River seasonings made their way far beyond the crab pot, showing up in dozens of recipes to give them a hint of the Chesapeake.

He didn't always need to reach for a can for authentic flavors of the Bay, though. A garden built a little too close to the edge of the water when we lived in Pasadena, Maryland, picked up a mist of salt spray when the waves kicked up. It wasn't enough to kill the tomatoes and basil growing there but was enough to inspire a tomato and basil soup.

Chesapeake Country and The Capital

Maryland
A Great Teacher's Chesapeake Fish Stew
Salt Spray Basil and Tomato Soup

Maryland's Eastern Shore
Saffron Crab Soup

Washington D.C.
Gorgonzola and Celery Soup
Mo Udall's Old Senate Bean Soup

Maryland A Great Teacher's Chesapeake Fish Stew

This soup is dedicated to Roger B. Farquhar of Sandy Springs, Maryland, one of my most dedicated, talented and nastiest editors. He once threw a typewriter at me. It missed but crashed through his second-floor office window and came oh-so-close to ruining the afternoon of a county judge walking below.

In a tiny weekly newspaper in a Maryland suburb of Washington, he also inflicted his journalistic values on *New York Times'* Robert Pear, *The Washington Post*'s Bob Woodward and Tom Shales, Knight Kiplinger of Kiplinger's Personal Finance and White House Press Secretary Ron Nessen.

This is an old family recipe that Roger had me cook for him.

Above: A Great Teacher's Chesapeake Fish Stew.
Photo by Paul Kitagaki, Jr.

Ingredients for 10 servings

Swordfish, cod or halibut, ½" cubes	¾ lb.
Shallots, chopped fine	3 T
Red onion, cut in ½" pieces	1 large
Fennel bulb, chopped medium	1½ cups
Diced canned tomatoes	1½ lbs.
Fish stock or clam juice	4 cups
Tomato paste	½ cup
Vermouth, dry, or white wine	2 cups
Bay leaf	1
Marjoram	½ t
Old Bay Seasoning	1 T
Oregano, chopped	1 t
Fennel fronds	½ cup
Lemon juice	2 T
Orange or lemon zest	2 T
Shrimp, large, shelled	1 lb.
Lobster or crab	1 lb.
Olive oil, extra virgin	2 oz.
Garlic, shaved	2 cloves
Fennel seed, toasted	2 t
Scallops	½ lb.
White pepper	½ t
Cilantro, chopped	½ cup

Optional

Pernod	2 T
Smoked hock or country ham	½ cup

Wash and bone fish. Set aside.

If using optional smoked ham hock, cut into small pieces.

Mince shallots and coarse-chop onions fine and fennel into ½" cubes.

In a heavy soup pot, heat olive oil over medium flame, add shallots, garlic, fennel seed and fennel, and cook until soft and lightly browned, about 6 to 8 minutes.

Add canned tomatoes, fish stock, tomato paste, vermouth, bay leaf, and seasonings.

Bring to a boil and cover. Lower heat and simmer for 15 minutes, stirring occasionally.

Add fennel fronds and fish; stir gently and simmer for 10 minutes.

Add scallops and Pernod. Simmer for 5 minutes.

Add lemon juice, orange or lemon zest, shrimp, smoked hock or country ham and crab meat. Stir very gently, simmering. AFTER 3 minutes, Remove bay leaf.

Sprinkle with cilantro.

Serve immediately.

Maryland Salt Spray Basil and Tomato Soup

If the gods are smiling, there is a chance that the crops of tomatoes and basil reach ripeness at the same time. However, when it does, you've got to be creative in coming up with ways to use the delicacies.

Based on experience—and years of dismal outcome as gardeners—we were shocked when three tiny basil starts blossomed into an enormous maze of basil three feet high and wider than our three Labs. What makes it even more unlikely is that the herb sprouted in our newly constructed raised planting boxes just four feet from the edge of the Chesapeake.

The salt spray generated when a brisk wind hits a high tide sends enough mist across the crops that there is sometimes a light coating of salt on the leaves. I, of course, predicted the immediate death of the crops, and of course, I was wrong. Perhaps I'll just stick to cooking.

If you want to make this after tomato season, good quality canned tomatoes can be used, as can the juice in the can.

Above: A sprig of culinary lavender sits atop a bowl of soup.
Photo by Andrew Schneider

Ingredients for 8 servings

Sweet onion, chopped fine	1½ cups
Olive oil	4 T
Garlic, minced fine	6 cloves
Tomatoes, chopped into small pieces	10 cups
Basil leaves, fresh, rolled together and sliced thin	40
Vinegar, cider, lemon flavored	4 T
Maggi seasoning	2 t
Dill, fresh, chopped fine	3 T
Chicken stock	6 cups
Kosher salt	2½ t
Black pepper	1 t
Whole basil leaves for garnish	8

In a heavy soup pot over a medium heat, add the chopped onions to the oil. Stir and cook until tender, but not browned (about 8-10 minutes).

Add garlic during the last two minutes and stir.

Add tomatoes and any juice they have created and stir.

Add the basil and vinegar, Maggi, dill, and stock. Stir, cover, and simmer for 15 minutes.

Add salt and pepper, stir, and cook for 5 more minutes.

Remove from heat and use an in-pot blender to smooth and blend the ingredients to whatever degree you prefer (I like it with a little body, so I don't blend it too smoothly).

Soup can be served chilled or hot. Garnish each bowl with a whole basil leaf.

Maryland's Eastern Shore Saffron Crab Soup

Tasty, yes. But there is little delicate about most crab soups. Some are cream based or loaded with tomatoes or stuffed like a chowder, easily a meal by themselves.

Not this crab concoction. This recipe is a modification from a soup made by the very patient 40-year girlfriend of a Chesapeake crabber from Cambridge, Maryland. Ernie didn't like it the first or second or even the third time that Connie made it for him. He wanted his crab stew to be something, he said, "that a man could get a bite into and know that he'd eaten something when he put the bowl down."

Ernie's doctor, a man he says "wouldn't know a crab if he was scratching for it," told the cranky waterman he would live to be nasty for a few more years if he cut down the heavy stews and chowders and stuck to clear broth when he needed a bowl of crab and liquid.

The clear liquid was tasty, but it wasn't until Connie, on her fourth attempt, threw in a handful of orzo, a rice-sized pasta that added some body to the broth, that Ernie finally stopped complaining. Within a couple of weeks, Ernie was taking credit for designing the soup.

Above: Saffron Crab Soup. Photo by Bill Lambrecht

Ingredients for 8 servings

Garlic, roasted	8 cloves
Shallots, roasted	2 large
Olive oil, extra virgin	4 T
Chesapeake blue crab or Dungeness crab meat	1 lb.
Fennel bulb, sliced ⅓" thick	1½ cups
Tomato, peeled, seeded, and chopped	2 cups
Old Bay seasoning	1 T
White pepper	⅓ t
Chicken or fish stock, clear	2 quarts
Madeira	½ cup
Saffron threads, toasted and crushed	1 t
Orzo pasta	8 ounces

(To give the uncooked orzo an interesting, nutty taste, bake on a foiled-lined pan for 20 minutes in a 350-degree oven.)

In an oven preheated to 400-degrees, place garlic and shallots covered in foil with 1 tablespoon olive oil. Cook for 45 minutes and set aside until cool.

Heat the remaining oil in a deep skillet or heavy wok. Add garlic, shallots and fennel. Cover and cook for 8 minutes.

Add tomatoes, seasoning (except saffron), and broth. Stir, cover, and simmer for about 10-12 minutes.

With an in-pot blender, blend until vegetables are finely chopped. Strain slowly into a fine mesh strainer. The tomato-fennel mixture can be used as a surprisingly good pasta sauce immediately or frozen for later use.

Return strained broth to pot. Add Madeira, saffron, crab meat, and orzo; cook for 7 minutes or until pasta is tender.

Washington, D.C. Gorgonzola and Celery Soup

A favorite on Capitol Hill that food historians say goes back at least a half-century. I usually serve it warm, but the French physician from whom this recipe was adapted served it chilled during Washington's scathing summers. The recipe came to me from a friend from Vietnam who was living in Washington.

Because of the egg yolks used in this recipe, it must be cooked thoroughly before chilling. If you're planning to serve chilled, reduce the amount of cheese by a little less than half.

Ingredients for 8 servings

Garlic, roasted	2 heads
Olive oil, extra virgin	4 T
Celery, chopped fine	4 cups
Leek (white part only), chopped fine	1 large
Flour, fine	3 T
Celery salt	1 t
Pepper, white	¼ t
Nutmeg, ground	1 t
Maggi seasoning	1 T
Chicken or vegetable stock	8 cups
Egg yolks	4
Whole milk or cream	2½ cups
Gorgonzola, dolce, cut in ½" pieces	10 oz.
Onion, sweet, minced	½ cup

Optional

Prosciutto, chiffonade and crisped	¼ cup

Cut the tops off garlic heads, drizzle with olive oil, wrap in foil, and bake at 400 degrees for 45 minutes. When cool, squeeze from papery skin and set aside.

Add olive oil to a heavy pot over medium heat. When hot, add garlic, celery, and leek. Stir well, cover and cook over medium heat until soft, about 8 to 10 minutes.

Add flour and seasonings. Stir while quickly adding stock to avoid lumps. Bring to light boil, cover, and simmer for 15 minutes.

Remove from heat and puree with an in-pot blender.

In a bowl, whisk egg yolks with milk; add two ladles of hot soup and the gorgonzola, preferably the Italian dolce or creamy style. Mix well and whisk egg mixture into pot. Heat but do not allow it to boil again.

When soup thickens slightly, serve garnished with a few celery leaves or prosciutto chiffonade cut into thin ribbons baked at 350-degrees until crisp.

Adjust seasoning. When reheating leftover soup, do not boil again.

Washington, DC — Mo Udall's Old Senate Bean Soup

The last time I checked, the soup being served in the Senate dining room was blander and made without onions, celery or garlic.

Mo Udall, then an Arizona congressman and Democratic presidential candidate, was able to get me the original recipe, or at least the one used from 1920 on.

"They changed it somewhere along the way and lots of us prefer the older version," Udall said. "Even cooks should know that if it's not broken, don't try to fix it."

Nonetheless, he added, his wife Tiger "always laced it with hot sauce."

I adapted this from an old recipe for U.S. Senate Bean Soup from Tiger Udall.

Ingredients for 8 servings

Sweet onions	2 medium
Celery, sliced thin	3 stalks
Garlic, shaved	3 cloves
Olive oil	2 Tbs
Navy beans, dried	2 lb.
Water or chicken stock	5 quarts
Smoked ham hocks	2
Salt and white pepper to taste	(start with 1 t white pepper, 2 t salt)

Rinse beans in cold, running water. Add water or chicken stock, beans and hocks into a large soup pot. Bring to boil, cover and cook over high heat 10 minutes. Turn off heat and let sit one hour. Uncover and return to heat. Simmer for 60 minutes until beans are soft. Uncover, return to heat, simmer 60 minutes until beans are soft, not mushy.

Sauté onions, celery and garlic until soft; do not allow to brown. Remove hocks, add onions, celery and garlic and stir.

Remove skin and bones from hocks. Slice meat into slivers and return to pot. Add more water or stock if needed. Simmer another 10-15 minutes. Adjust seasonings and serve.

Andy and son Patrick talk with U.S. Rep. Mo Udall, D-Ariz. and his wife Ella "Tiger" Udall outside a campaign event in New Hampshire in 1976.

V

The Northeast

1974-1982

Newsweek

Associated Press

New Hampshire Times

*Schneider pulls a lobster from the pot in New Hampshire in the 1970s.
Photo by Patrick Schneider*

The Northeast

New England always had a special place in Andy's heart. The fall leaves, the White Mountains, the craggy coastline, the picturesque villages, the first-in-the-nation presidential primary: All played a part. But I suspect it was the sugaring shacks that sealed the deal. Maple sugar and syrup show up in multiple recipes as that special something that makes the dish.

Living in New England was not always idyllic.

While reporting for the Associated Press there, Andy almost got suspended for sending out a bulletin that said a Quebec Nordiques player had scored a hat check against the Boston Bruins. He organized coverage of one of the largest mass arrests in U.S. history during protests at the Seabrook Nuclear Power Plant construction site in New Hampshire, then got sent by the wire service to Three Mile Island in Pennsylvania to cover the nation's worst nuclear disaster. (At the University of Massachusetts at Lowell, he had earned a certificate allowing him to operate a nuclear power plant.)

Below: Schneider, wearing a gas mask, and an AP photographer catch their breath during an anti-nuclear protest at the Seabrook Nuclear Power Plant construction site in New Hampshire in 1977. Photo by Patrick Schneider

He broke the news that Miss Lillian Carter had told New Hampshire voters at a campaign stop for her son, the president, that she'd like to hire someone to kill Iranian Ayatollah Khomeini. And he was stabbed with an ice pick in Newburyport, Massachusetts, while investigating interstate shipments of hazardous waste that were being dumped in New England. His attacker was never caught.

In the summer, lobster boils were a staple. The pots were loaded with corn and potatoes prepared to bubble as soon as the car loaded with crustaceans from Maine or Massachusetts crested the hill. In the long, snowy winters, his Yankee neighbor in Contoocook, New Hampshire, shared her secrets for pot roast and soups. His treks to Quebec to gather string on an alleged nuclear weapons manufacturer produced Canadian culinary adventures.

As always, he made sure the people he cared for were well fed.

Kimberly Marlowe Hartnett, a former AP colleague who became a dear friend, recalled that when the siege at Seabrook ended with the arrest of more than 1,400 people, Andy cajoled the AP bureau chief into taking everyone out to dinner at "some Ye Old Fancy New England Inn kinda place."

"We were a big group, all sitting at a couple of long tables—reporters, photographers, local and national folks," Hartnett said. "We'd been existing on fast food for days—and some people were whining, I guess—and so Andy arranged for the waiters to bring in bags full of McDonald's meals to the tables before the good stuff showed up. It got a big laugh, and of course, all of the food—McD's and the good stuff—got eaten."

New England dumping: In between calamities, he took full advantage of the terroir.

fights 'poison haulers' who ...astes in woods and fields

Investigators, if they're very lucky, eventually will find remnants of the cargo in abandoned gravel pits, pastures, or ravines.

Police say those seeking the "broker's" services usually are in the industrial belt of New Jersey, Pennsylvania and Delaware, but they also suspect there are many dumpers from southern New England.

At loading docks, trucks display newly issued magnetic signs listing names of legitimate-sounding waste disposal companies. As the drums are loaded, manifests showing cargo and destination are prepared. Skull and crossbone placards warning of hazardous cargo are attached to the trucks.

Some companies, judging from dumpsites found by authorities, carefully package and label wastes. Others make no pretense to follow detailed regulations. The trucks are crammed with rusty, often leaky drums of unidentified chemicals.

The charade of legality ends outside the factory gate. The driver stops, removes the phony company signs from the doors, the warnings from the trailers and substitutes a bogus manifest.

Now, instead of reflecting 50 drums of poison, the truck is shown to be hauling anything from sawdust to marshmallow topping.

Truckers say a manifest is accepted at face value, and a bogus one will get most truckers through a police check or safety inspection.

One story has it that a Massachusetts state trooper spotted a steamy liquid dripping from a truck. Acid from a rusty drum had eaten through the straps holding the containers in place. The trooper flagged the truck down, told the driver his cargo was leaking and drove off without getting out of his cruiser.

It's the fear of what they carry, not the thought of getting caught, that prompts truckers to dump their cargo as quickly as possible.

Medical experts say the chemicals, when improperly handled, can cause fits of coughing, uncontrolled bowel movements, difficulty in breathing or death.

Drivers say it's worth the risk. The money is rumored to be two or three times the regular rates — and paid in cash. Some truckers say there's as much business available as a driver wants if he's trusted.

Once on the road, the driver checks his instructions for meeting a contact. Investigators say the contact system makes it difficult to tail a truck. It also keeps the trucker from knowing the exact location of the dump he will be led to.

New England

Maine
Screw the Admiral Lobster Stew

New Hampshire
Civil War Baked Beans
Milne's Lobster Stew
Miss Lillian's Peanut Soup
Pot Roast Au Vin

Quebec
Black Ice Lobster Quebec
Coq au Vin Pacific

Maine Screw the Admiral Lobster Stew

It is said that the recipe for this lobster stew has been passed from sailor to sailor for years among the top NCOs who served at Brunswick Naval Air Station on Maine's coast. As the story goes, the stew was first served at a party of senior Navy enlisted men and a gaggle of bosun's mates several decades ago to soothe their bruised egos after the base commander, an admiral with no sense of humor and unhappy over some minor infractions of the rules, canceled all leaves and vacations. On a Saturday afternoon in July, dozens of the sailors and assorted friends gathered at a place called Basin Cove. The cove is at the end of the finger of land near the base that follows Harpswell Sound into the Atlantic. Somehow, 80 pounds of lobster from the Admiral's mess also showed up. Thus the spirit of this recipe was born.

Above: Screw the Admiral Lobster Stew. Photo by Marcia Myers

Ingredients for 10 one-cup servings; can also be main course for four

Lobsters	6 lbs in the shell
Butter, sweet	4 oz.
Onions, sweet, finely chopped	1 large
Fennel bulb, sliced thin	1 cup
Yukon potato in ½" cubes	1 cup
Garlic, shaved	3 cloves
Sweet sherry or Madeira	1 cup
Lobster broth	5 cups
Milk, whole	5 cups
Dill, parsley, and thyme, fresh	3 sprigs each
Kosher salt, coarse	¼ t
White pepper	¼ t
Ginger, ground or fresh	¼ t
Vanilla extract	½ t

Optional

Sweet corn, kernels removed	6 ears

Boil the lobster "until it turns sun red," the old-timers said. More precisely, dunk the lobsters headfirst into a rolling boil of salted water and cover. Cooking time varies by the size of the lobsters. 10 minutes for a 2-pound lobster; 5-6 minutes for a 1-pound lobster. Save the cooking broth.

Remove, cool, shell, and cut into 1-inch chunks.

In a large heavy pot, melt butter and add onions, fennel bulb, potatoes, and garlic. Stirring, cook for three minutes until slightly soft. Do not allow it to brown.

Add sherry or Madeira and stir well.

Strain lobster broth and add to the pot. Boil lightly for about 10 minutes or until potatoes are cooked.

Slowly add milk or cream (equal in amount to the lobster broth). For example, if you get 5 cups of strained broth, add 5 cups of milk or cream.

Tie sprigs of herbs with butcher's string or wrap in cheesecloth and add to the pot with sea salt, white pepper, ginger, vanilla extract, and lobster meat.

Simmer lightly for five minutes. Remove from heat, let sit 10 minutes, and serve

Note: The Navy recipe calls for heavy cream and half-and-half. Whole milk works almost as well. A Navy cook who said he was at one of the early bosun's feasts told me that to make the broth richer, cook the shells after the meat is removed. He said that the bodies of the lobsters should be cooked with the "innards intact." Bring enough water to cover the lobster shells to a boil, cover and simmer "a good hour or more" and strain carefully. This can be done beforehand.

*Meats sizzle on the grill.
Photo by Andrew Schneider*

New Hampshire Civil War Baked Beans

This recipe is the result of a heated, oft-repeated battle between a Bostonian and a Georgian in my old kitchen in New Hampshire. It takes the best of several regional differences and tosses them into the pot. But it is easy to modify with your own favorites.

One point to consider is where to get the smoky flavor. Thin slivers of country ham, crisp pig skin or pieces of smoked pork can be used. If those aren't available or if you're trying to keep the fat down, liquid smoke can be used in very small quantities.

I use smoked pasilla chile, or chipotle, which is a smoked, dried jalapeno, ground into a powder in my local spice shop. It can be found in many groceries as the popularity of Hispanic cooking grows. It adds multiple layers of flavor without too much heat.

Above: Civil War Baked Beans. Photo by Tony Cutraro

Ingredients for 15 servings

Great Northern white beans	8 oz.
Red kidney beans	8 oz.
Pinto beans	8 oz.
Olive oil, extra virgin	2 T
Thick bacon or pork back, sliced in 1" pieces	8 oz.
Sweet onion, cut in ½" pieces	1 large
Sweet green peppers, cut in ½" pieces	2 large
Sweet red or yellow peppers cut in ½" pieces	2 large
Garlic, shaved	6 cloves
Plum tomatoes whole, peeled, canned	1 lb.
Juice from tomatoes or V-8	½ cup
Worcestershire sauce	2 T
Mustard seed, yellow	2 T
Cumin seed	½ T
Celery seed	2 t
Maple sugar	2 T
Barbecue sauce	½ cup
Liquid smoke flavoring	½ t
Chipotle chile, powdered	1 t
Salt and pepper to taste	

Optional

Country ham, cooked, slivered	6 oz.
Molasses	4 T

As with any bean dish, pick them over carefully, toss out the debris, and soak overnight. If you're in a hurry, cover the beans with cold water in a heavy pot, plus an inch or two, and bring to a boil for 4 minutes. Remove from heat and let sit for 90 minutes.

Rinse beans well in cold water and drain. Return to the pot, cover with cold water, and bring to boil. Reduce heat to medium-low and simmer for 30 minutes or until beans are tender.

Meanwhile, into a Dutch oven, over medium heat, add either the bacon or fat back in the olive oil. Cook until crisp and remove for later use.

Add to the remaining bacon fat the onions and sweet pepper; sauté about 3 minutes or until soft. Add garlic. Stir and cook for another minute.

Add the canned tomatoes, meat, the beans plus ¼ cup of the bean liquid, the reserved tomato juice, and all the seasonings but the salt, which is added last to keep the beans from getting tough.

Stir well, cover, and cook in an oven preheated to 325 degrees for 3 hours, stirring every hour. Or cook over low simmer on stove top, stirring every few minutes. When beans are tender, add salt, check seasonings, stir, and serve.

Above: Schneider holds a perfectly cooked lobster in his St. Louis kitchen, circa 2002. Photo by Kathy Best

New Hampshire — Milne's Lobster Stew

Jon Milne of Exeter, New Hampshire, is a stubborn granite head with a heart of gold, as long as you don't talk politics with him. He's also a purist and refuses to let his recipe for lobster stew be, as he puts it, "messed with."

Although the temptation to swap the half and half for milk and add just a sprinkle of spices is strong, even stronger is my belief that if it isn't broken, don't fix It.

This is not broken. It is simple to the point of being poetic. The flavor improves after sitting. Your willpower will be rewarded.

Above: Lobsters steam in a pot. Photo by Andrew Schneider

Milne's Lobster Stew. Photo by Marcia Myers

Ingredients for 8 servings

Lobster meat	4-5 lbs.
Butter, unsalted	4 oz
Half and half	64 oz.

Figure 8 ounces of meat out of a 1-pound lobster.

Boil or steam the lobster. Boil a "chicken" or one-pounder for no more than 5 minutes or steam for 10 minutes.

Let cool and remove meat.

Cut tail into chunks and pick out claw and leg meat.

In a large saucepan, sauté meat in butter over a low heat for just a few minutes as the butter thickens; stir constantly. Add half and half; heat slowly over very low heat for 45 minutes,

Remove from heat. Let sit for 2-3 hours.

Reheat slowly. Do not boil.

Above: Andy and daughter Kelly Schneider hold giant lobsters outside his Capitol Hill home in Washington, D.C. Photo by Kathy Best

New Hampshire — Miss Lillian's Peanut Soup
Adapted from a recipe from Lillian Carter of Plains, Georgia

President Jimmy Carter's mother was more popular than her son.

It was three weeks before the end of the New Hampshire silly season, the nation's first presidential primary. All the candidates had taken their best shot at the Granite State votes and had moved on to more significant political battlefields in Florida, Ohio and California.

But every four years, someone proves that no one can afford to dis New Hampshire's spoiled voters, so the candidates' wives, daughters and mothers had been enlisted to flood the state to keep their loved ones' names before the pampered electorate.

It was a snowy Tuesday night. But the heat was up at the Bow Men's Club, a brick building about a mile from Concord, as the crusty old men were warming up to Jimmy Carter's mother, Miss Lillian, who was doing the honors.

Above: Miss Lillian's Peanut Soup. Photo by Pamela Baker-Masson

The all-male audience was eating up the nation's first mom's view of the rest of the world. But her traveling press corps, most unhappy at being assigned to cover the surrogates, had headed for the kitchen while she spoke, leaving me as the sole reporter in the hall.

During the question-and-answer session, Miss Lillian was asked how she would "handle fanatics" like Ayatollah Khomeini.

"If I had a million dollars to spare I'd look for someone to kill him," she said.

I called in the quote, which evoked cheers from the crowd, to my bosses at the AP, who instantly put it on the wire, resulting in headlines around the world and a headache for her son.

I feared that the story would doom my chances of ever getting Miss Lillian to share her recipe for peanut soup. She lectured me on the campaign trail that it was sinful to even consider making it from peanut butter but would never part with details.

But within days of the Ayatollah story, one of her personal light-blue envelopes from Plains, Georgia, arrived in the mail.

Sometimes you've got to stay out of the kitchen to get a good recipe.

With a little change to the seasonings, here's Miss Lillian's recipe:

Ingredients for 10 servings

Dried peanuts, unsalted, ground fine	
(roast in oven, then cool before grinding)	3½ cups
Butter, sweet	3 T
Sweet onion	
(Ms. Lillian liked Georgia's Vidalia), chopped fine	¾ cup
Flour	3 T
Chicken stock	8 cups
Celery salt	½ t
White pepper	½ t
Kosher salt,	1½ t
Lemon juice	2½ t
Cream, half and half or whole milk	2½ cups
Tabasco to taste	¼ t

Garnish

Whole peanuts	½ cup
Cilantro	1 bunch

Toast whole peanuts lightly at 325 degrees for 5 minutes or until browned and fragrant. Use care because all nuts go from brown to charred very quickly. Set aside ½ cup for garnish.

Grind remaining peanuts in a spice mill, blender, or food processor. Take care not to overgrind or the peanuts will clump into a glob. A rough chop on the peanuts is fine because the soup is blended at the end. (Miss Lillian said that using peanut butter "gave the soup the very wrong taste.")

In a heavy pot over medium heat, melt the sweet butter, but do not allow butter to brown.

Add the onion and sauté until soft and very lightly browned (about 4-5 minutes.)

Stir in the finely chopped peanuts and sauté for a minute. Lower heat, add flour, stir well, and cook for 2 minutes.

Add chicken stock, lemon juice and seasonings, bring to boil, stir well, cover, and simmer for 20 minutes.

In a bowl, add cream, half and half or whole milk. Whisk two cups of liquid from the pot, one cup at a time. Then pour liquid back into the pot.

Cook over low heat for five minutes. Do not boil again.

Use an in-pot blender to smooth out the soup. Check seasonings.

For garnish, serve topped with a heaping teaspoon or more of toasted peanuts and/or cilantro.

Schneider interviews presidential candidate Jimmy Carter on one of his campaign trips to New Hampshire in 1975. Photo by Patrick Schneider

New Hampshire Pot Roast Au Vin

"It was a dark and stormy night" would be a way to explain why we created this comforting meal. But it is actually a blend of pot roast recipes from a wonderful woman from Miami, Minnie Sternberg, and a lovely lady from New Hampshire, Mary O'Carroll.

My great-grandmother Minnie Sternberg believed that great pot roast should be cooked with sweet fruit, so when she was living in the South she added mango, prunes, sometimes figs, and always a bit of brandy to the pot. Thirty years later, Mary O'Carroll, a premier cook in Contoocook, N.H., showed me the value of adding maple sugar, dried apples and cherries and some fruity wine to her Yankee pot.

If using short ribs, have the butcher cut ribs into 2-inch pieces. Substitute any fruit that you like, but remember that dried fruit holds up better during cooking.

This recipe can be cooked in the oven, but I often cook it over a low heat on the stovetop until fork-tender.

Ingredients for 10 servings

Olive oil	¼ cup
Boneless chuck roast or short ribs	4 lbs.
Coarse sea salt	2 t
Coarse black pepper	½ t
Thyme, dried	3 T
Rosemary	4 sprigs
Onions, yellow or sweet, coarsely chopped	3 cups
Carrots, large, julienned or cut into ½" pieces	4
Shallots, chopped large	1 cup
Garlic, chopped large	6 cloves
Mushrooms, white or wild, halved	1 lb.
Flour	¼ cup
Beef or mushroom broth enriched with porcini bouillon cubes	2 cups
Red wine	3½ cups
Italian tomatoes, diced or whole, with liquid	3 cups
Smoked pasilla chile, powdered	½ t
Maggi seasoning	1 T
Maple sugar, powered	1 T
Dried cherries or cranberries, in wine or brandy	⅔ cup
Dried apple or apricot, soaked in wine or brandy	½ cup

Above left: Pot Roast Au Vin. Photo by Tony Cutraro

Mix porcini bouillon cubes with hot water or beef stock and set aside.

Preheat the oven to 350 degrees.

Heat 2 T of olive oil in a large heavy pot or Dutch oven over a high heat. Salt and pepper the roast or short ribs. Rub seasonings well and place meat in the pot fat side down. Sear the meat until well browned, about 2 to 3 minutes per side. Remove the meat and set aside.

Lower heat and add remaining olive oil to the pot, then add the onions and carrots. Stir and cook over medium heat until lightly browned, about 5 minutes. Add the shallots, garlic, and mushroom. Stir gently and cook for another 3 or 4 minutes.

Sprinkle in the flour. Stir and cook for about 1 minute. Slowly add broth, wine, tomatoes, seasonings, spices, and maple sugar; bring to a simmer.

Put the roast back in the pot, cover, and cook for 2 hours over low heat. After 1 hour, add dried fruit and the wine it was soaking in. Turn meat.

Cook meat until internal temperature reaches 145 degrees for medium to 170 degrees for well done.

Transfer the roast to a cutting board and cover loosely with foil. Remove the vegetables, cover, and keep warm.

Thickly slice the meat across the grain about ½" thick.

Place meat and vegetables on a platter.

Return the cooking pot to high heat and skim excess fat off sauce. Boil, stirring and skimming frequently, until sauce is thickened.

Remove herb sprigs and adjust seasoning of sauce if needed. Strain and serve in a gravy boat.

Quebec Black Ice Lobster Quebec

Black ice can make even a bad day worse. The two lanes of the small road south of Montreal were narrowed to little more than one by the deep snow. What little road remained was covered with a glaze of black ice.

We sat by a driveway to a tiny cottage deciding what to do when suddenly the stillness of the valley was shattered with the screech of metal on metal. A small van skidded, fishtailed into the snow-covered bank and then into the trunk of a large tree.

Neither of the van's two passengers, both professors from McGill University, was hurt. But they bemoaned a leaking crack in a tank holding six live lobsters.

The van was manhandled back on the road, but because of the black ice, no one was going anywhere.

Two elderly sisters invited all to spend the night in their snug but warm cottage. The professors offered their lobsters and we donated the cognac. The following recipe comes from what the sisters threw together that night.

Above: Black Ice Lobster Quebec. Photo by Marcia Myers

Ingredients for 6 servings

Lobsters, live, 2 lbs.	6
Shallot, sliced thin	2 large
Butter	4 T
Cognac	6 T
Light cream	1 cup
White pepper	¼ t
Kosher salt	½ T

Plunge the lobsters, headfirst, into a large pot of boiling salted water. For two-pounders, boil at least seven minutes. Remove and cool enough to handle.

Meanwhile, lightly sauté the shallots in butter.

Remove from the heat when slightly brown; add cognac, cream, and seasonings, Stir well. Do not boil.

Using either a very large knife or large kitchen shears, cut the lobsters lengthwise and crack the claws. Scoop out any eggs and the green tomalley (liver).

Lay meat side up in a large baking pan, spoon on the cream mixture, and grill beneath an oven broiler for about 4 minutes or until lobster is slightly browned.

Quebec Coq au Vin Pacific

My father, a trained cook, would make his version of this dish a couple of times a year on special occasions. I remember him saying that he hoped his old French cooking instructor never found out what he was doing. It was years later that I learned what he meant.

I was on an assignment in Saint-Vallier, a river town a bit east of Quebec City. The grandmother of the man I was interviewing was well known for her cooking skills, and she was making Coq au Vin that weekend. I told her of my father's comments. She laughed and said, I would understand when we got to a new nearby farm, where she was buying the birds.

The traditional recipe translates into cock or rooster and wine, she said, which is why it would simmer for hours until tender enough to eat. The best my father could get was an old hen from the kosher butcher that, while not traditional, still tasted great.

I call it Pacific Coq Au Vin because I learned on the Oregon coast to add various wild mushrooms, dried Rainier cherries soaked in apple brandy and even slices of apples. With or without the Northwest twist, it is a classic worth trying. I would keep the wild mushrooms in any case.

Above: Pacific Coq au Vin. Photo by Christian Masson

Ingredients for 6 to 8 servings

Garlic, roasted	2 heads
Shallots, roasted	6 medium
Olive oil	6 T
Wild mushrooms, halved	1 lb.
Dried cherries	½ cup
Brandy for soaking cherries.	½ cup
Bacon or pork belly thickly sliced	8 oz.
Butter	2 T
Yellow onion, finely chopped	1 cup
Chicken legs, thighs, and breast with skin on	4 lbs.
Salt and pepper	to taste
French (nante) carrots julienned	18
Fennel, chopped	½ cup
Cognac or apple brandy	⅓ cup
Burgundy or any good red wine	4 cups
Rich chicken stock	3 cups
Artichoke hearts, quartered	18
Tomato paste	½ cup
Mustard powder	½ t
Maggi seasoning	2 T
Thyme	6 fresh 3-inch sprigs
Rosemary	3 fresh 3-inch sprigs
Nutmeg, fresh	1 t
Flour	4 T

Preheat the oven to 400 degrees and cut tops off garlic heads and shallots. Drizzle with 1½ tablespoons olive oil, wrap in foil, and roast for 45 minutes. Then set aside to cool.

Chop mushrooms; set aside.

Meanwhile, soak dried cherries in brandy.

Lay bacon or pork belly into a cold Dutch oven or heavy enameled pan. Turn the heat to medium-low and cook slowly until the bacon or pork is crisp. Remove meat and set aside drippings.

In the same pan, add 2 tablespoons olive oil and onions. Sauté and stir occasionally until soft and lightly browned. Set aside.

Season the chicken on all sides with salt and pepper. Add the reserved bacon fat and 1 ½ tablespoons olive oil to pan. Brown the chicken over medium heat on all sides, about six to eight minutes. Remove from the pot and set aside.

Return onions to pan. Add 1 tablespoon olive oil to the pan add the carrots and fennel, cooking over medium heat until soft, about 5 minutes.

Squeeze the garlic and shallots out of their papery skins. Stir into the pot.

Return browned chicken to the pot and add the cooked bacon or pork belly cut into ½" thick pieces. Add mushrooms and gently stir.

Add the cognac and ignite. Carefully stir until the flame dies down.

Finish with wine, chicken stock, artichokes, tomato paste, and cherries. (Discard or drink brandy used for soaking.)

Add salt and pepper, mustard powder, and Maggi. Tie springs of thyme and rosemary into a bunch and add to pot along with nutmeg

Cover and simmer on medium-low heat for about 45 minutes or until chicken is tender.

Remove chicken from the pot and increase heat to reduce sauce by about a third.

In a bowl or mixing cup, blend 4 tablepoons flour and 2 tablespoons butter together. Gradually add 1 cup of sauce, missing well. Pour mixture back into pot and stir well over high heat until sauce thickens. Lower heat to low and return chicken, cooking 3 minutes or until chicken is hot.

Cover until ready and serve with buttered egg noodles, farro, or spaetzle.

VI

The Northwest

1996-2017

The Northwest

West Coast. East Coast. Mountains. Saltwater. The pull of each was always strong, and deciding among them was always hard, which explains why Andy and I kept bouncing around. A brief stop in the Midwest only underscored the allure of the coasts, especially during tornado season. Although Andy grew up in hurricane country, he was not amused by the electric light shows of a St. Louis thunderstorm, especially at night when a twister could drop from the darkness unseen.

The editor of the Oregonian in Portland had been trying for years to lure Andy away from Washington, D.C., to join her staff. He finally said yes and, in between investigations of a broken child abuse prevention system and the armed hunt for precious mushrooms in an Oregon national forest, he fell in love with the cuisine of the Pacific Northwest and the spectacular coasts of Oregon and Washington.

Salmon, of course, was the centerpiece. I gave him his first smoker when he lived in Portland–he claimed it's why he eventually married me. He became a master at smoking slabs of king and sockeye over alder with a rub he concocted from Pernod, dark rum, fresh dill, maple sugar (of course), mustard seed, salt and lemon pepper.

Salmon also appeared in hash, in filets bought right off the boats at Fishermen's Terminal in Seattle, and poached in wine.

Seattle, where the scent of the sea perfumes the morning air, lured Andy north, where he joined me at the *Seattle Post-Intelligencer* for the first of his two stints at the feisty morning newspaper. It didn't hurt that the *P-I*'s editor and publisher, J.D. Alexander, was a gourmand who talked food with him and approved expenses that included Andy's purchase of white truffles for a story he did on the pungent fungi.

Andy did some amazing stories for the *P-I*. He and partner Mike Barber got innocent people out of jail after proving that evidence in an alleged child sex ring in Wenatchee, Wash., was based on lies and bad science. He also disclosed the international "honey laundering" business, using import records and sophisticated testing of pollen to prove that much of the sweet, golden liquid sold on store shelves comes from China and isn't honey at all.

Between stories, he could often be found at Pike Place Market, Seattle's renowned 115-year-old farmers market that draws fresh food purveyors from the coast and the drier environs east of the Cascade Mountains. The bounty on offer included a dozen kinds of mushrooms, fish, crabs and mollusks, succulent fresh berries, Rainier, tart and Bing cherries, sweet Walla Walla onions, fresh-from-the garden veggies and spectacular dahlias, sunflowers, delphiniums and other flowers grown by Hmong farmers.

All but the flowers ended up in his soup pots and roasting pans. And some of it was sent back East. When he learned that the Pacific Northwest was home to the marionberry, he couldn't resist cooking up a batch of jam to send to friends in Washington, D.C., where the notorious Marion Barry still ruled as mayor.

Most of the time, Andy was happy buying what he needed for the kitchen. But when he learned that a Washington beach where we vacationed was a prime hunting ground for Pacific razor clams, he bought a license—for me. He was great at spotting the tell-tale squirts of a lurking clam and was standing by with a pot and a recipe for razor clam chowder when I successfully captured one.

Low tide brings out the Pacific razor clammers on Copalis Beach in Washington state. Photo by Andrew Schneider

Andy's managing editor at the P-I was David McCumber, who loved a great story and great food just as much as Andy. The two worked together on a story they would later turn into a book, disclosing the widespread asbestos poisoning of the residents of Libby, Montana, by the W.R. Grace Co. Andy stumbled on the story while investigating the environmental legacy of hard-rock mining in Montana. The heroic whistleblowers in Libby and the federal environmental experts sent to help them after publication of Andy's initial Libby investigation became lifelong friends.

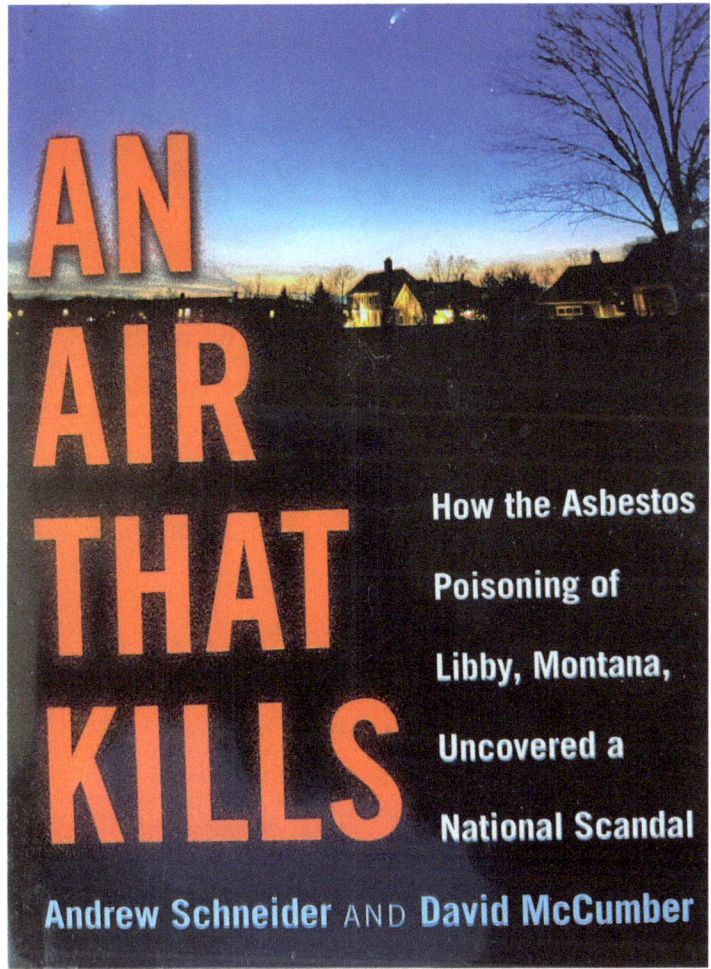

The cover of the book Schneider and his editor at the Seattle Post-Intelligencer, David McCumber, wrote on the asbestos poisoning of miners and their families by the W.R. Grace Co. in Libby, Montana.

Working on the story, Andy fell in love with Montana—from the Cabinet Mountains surrounding Libby in the northwest corner of the state to the Bitterroot Mountains south of Missoula. Huckleberries grew wild on the mountain slopes. Bison and cattle grazed on the prairies. And geese and ducks stopped over on their spring and winter commutes.

After deciding to leave our Seattle jobs, we moved to Montana, not knowing it would be for the last year of Andy's life.

The Northwest

Montana
Duck Breasts with Huckleberry Sauce
A Montana Standing Prime Rib Roast

Oregon
Fog-Bound Spinach Soup
Forest Wild Mushroom Soup
Scallop Confetti Soup

Washington State
D.B. Cooper Salmon Hash
Doctor's Daughter's Poached Salmon

Montana Duck Breasts with Huckleberry Sauce

Adapted from great meals eaten in Whitefish and Missoula, Montana, where pickers fight the bears for huckleberries. If you cannot get huckleberries—which is often the case—you can use huckleberry syrup, but cut the amount of sugar in half.

The sauce works well on any white meat or on salmon and halibut.

Ingredients for four servings

Duck breasts (boned with skin on)	4
Shallot, chopped fine	1 large
Huckleberries	4 oz.
Maple sugar, powdered or crystal	2 T
Maple liquor or brandy	3 T
Chicken or veal stock, strong	2 oz.
Butter	2 T
Sea salt	½ t
White pepper, coarse	½ t

Preheat the oven to 400 degrees. Using a very sharp knife, score skin down to flesh in a diagonal pattern.

Heat a heavy-bottomed sauté pan or iron skillet on high until until hot.

Add duck breasts, skin side down. Sear over medium heat until skin is well browned, 4 or 5 minutes, then reduce heat to moderately low.

Flip over and cook the second side until flesh is firm to the touch, about 3-5 minutes. This will deliver duck cooked medium rare. (If breasts are large, use meat thermometer and cook to 155 degrees.)

Place duck in an oven preheated to heat to 225 degrees. Remove all but 3 tablespoons of the duck fat from the skillet.

Add the shallots and sauté for 1 minute.

Add huckleberries, maple sugar, brandy, or maple liquor.

Stir well and bring to a boil to reduce by half in volume.

Add the stock and simmer until again reduced by half in volume.

Whisk in the butter and remove from the heat. Season with salt and pepper, as needed. Remove the duck breasts from the oven. Spoon the sauce over the duck breasts and serve.

Drummond, Montana, is known as the biggest bull shipper in the state. Metzger's Cow Lot ships cattle mainly from Montana to the Midwest via rail and truck.
Photo by Andrew Schneider

Montana Standing Prime Rib Roast

It's called a standing roast because it contains rib bones that act as a natural rack. However, for the ease of carving you might ask your butcher to remove the bones and then tie them back on. You want to do this because cooking with the bones attached will add a measurable amount of additional flavor.

When determining how large a roast to buy, figure on feeding two people from one rib. For example, 12 people can be served a more than ample amount of beef from a roast with six ribs.

A friend who lives in the Bitterroot Valley always dry ages or "conditions" his beef to increase flavor and tenderness. He starts with a roast that's graded USDA Prime (but USDA Choice can be used, he admits), he cleans the beef, dries it carefully, wraps it in cheesecloth, and refrigerates it for a week or 10 days at a consistent 38-40 degrees.

He cuts away any crust that forms and cooks it.

Yes, it's a pain and my friends at the USDA say don't try this at home unless you learn how to do it right. But I think it's worth it because the results are oh so good. Of course, you can always order it from a high-end butcher if money is no object.

Ingredients for 12 servings

Bone-in prime rib roast	6 lbs.
Garlic, cut into thick slivers	8 cloves
Bourbon or dark rum	½ cup
Kosher salt	4 T
Black pepper, coarse	
Mustard, coarse	1 T
Rosemary, dried or fresh, chopped fine	1½ T

Remove roast from refrigerator and let sit for 90 minutes to two hours. Preheat the oven to 450 degrees.

Using a sharp, small knife, cut eight or 10 slits into the fat of the roast and insert large slivers of garlic (about four pieces from each clove).

Rub bourbon into the roast and combine salt, pepper, mustard, and rosemary; apply heavily to the roast and press into meat. Place fat up on a rack in a shallow pan, put in the oven, and roast for 15 minutes. Reduce heat to 325 degrees and roast for another 15 minutes a pound or until internal temperature reaches 130 to 135 degrees for medium rare or 140 degrees for medium. Rely on an accurate thermometer rather than the clock.

Let stand for at least 20 minutes, covered lightly with foil. If you must hold it before carving and serving, return to the oven, which now has the heat off. I've done it for as long as an hour with only a slight increase in doneness.

Oregon Fog-Bound Spinach Soup

Sometimes a good recipe can get better by accident, and this is one where that happened. The original recipe, which came from a small inn outside Alba, Italy, had a few more ingredients and a few more steps. Fog bound in a beach house in Yachats on the Oregon coast and unable to begin to find the road, let alone a store, we made do with what we had. This skimpier version looks better—far more vivid color—and I think tastes better.

Above: Fog-Bound Spinach Soup. Photo by Jackie Koszczuk

Ingredients for 4 servings

Olive oil, extra virgin	1 t
Bacon, thick-sliced, cut in ¼" pieces	2 strips
Garlic, minced	2 cloves
Green onions, white part only, cut ¼" thick	6
Plum tomatoes, cut in ¼" pieces	3
Chicken stock	5 cups
White pepper	¼ t
Kosher salt	½ t
Mustard powder	¼ t
Spinach, fresh, torn into bite-sized pieces	2 cups

Pour olive oil into a heavy saucepan and heat over a medium flame.

Add bacon and cook slowly until well browned, about 5 minutes.

Add onions and cook until soft and lightly brown, about 7 to 8 minutes.

Add garlic and cook until slightly browned, about 2 minutes. Do not allow garlic to burn.

Add tomatoes and stir. Cook for 3 more minutes or until tomatoes are softened.

Add stock and seasoning, bring to boil, reduce heat to simmer, cover, and cook for 10 minutes.

Add spinach; stir until wilted.

Oregon Forest Wild Mushroom Soup

I adapted this from the recipe of Betty Olsen and her sidekick Elise. The two widows had hunted and collected exceptional mushrooms in the wild national forests of southern Oregon for decades. It was this feisty duo that warned me that if you take a mycologist to dinner you better count on having something with mushrooms in it.

Above: Forest Wild Mushroom Soup. Photo by Lore Postman

I met the ladies as I was tromping through the Deschutes National Forest, about 100 miles north of the California state line. It was just after Labor Day, and I was sent to the woods to report on what had triggered a violent rampage among Lao, Thai and Vietnamese commercial mushroom hunters. In the preceding week, two had been shot dead and seven others wounded in makeshift mushroom camps around Crescent Lake Junction. The woods were teeming with hundreds of hunters carrying government-issued permits to pick matsutakes or "matsies."

Many cooks consider this culinary fungus the elite of true wild mushrooms. Its scent of pine mixed with a tinge of cinnamon has been revered by the Japanese for centuries as a symbol of health, wealth, and virility and reserved only for members of the Imperial Court. Today, matsies are prestigious gifts that Japan's ruthlessly competitive business executives reserve for special customers.

During the picking season, matsutakes can be found in farmers markets throughout the Pacific Northwest for $25 to $50 a pound But in Japan and other Asian countries, a single flawless fungus can bring $500 or more.

A forest service ranger told me that the commercial collecting of matsutakes is a rough, big business with a lot of money involved. He pointed to clusters of "mushroom brokers" sitting under hastily erected blue tarps. Their collapsible tables held delicate scales, a box or bag of cash, and express air shipping packaging. That's why many of the pickers tote pistols along with their collection baskets, the federal forest cop explained.

We're armed, too, Betty told me. She pointed to an ancient but still gleaming rifle secured to a rack just inside the door of the equally old Winnebago motorhome. From a Dutch oven, suspended over the orange embers of a dying wood fire, she ladled out a bowl of the fragrant, still steaming mushroom soup. No matsutakes, Betty said, but it had six other mushrooms and was wonderful.

In following Betty's recipe, it would be nice to select your mushrooms by taste, but the reality of what's available in the market or growing from an old log will usually dictate what you use. There are scores of edible wild mushrooms, but the tastiest and the easiest to find are shiitake, chanterelles, oyster, black trumpet and, if it's the right season, some morels. Fresh porcini border on the impossible to get on a regular basis, but if you can locate some and are willing to pay $30 to $50 a pound, you're sure to find it's worth it.

Commercially grown mushrooms like white button or baby bellas are your fast choice in flavor. If these are all that are available, increase the amount of dried porcini, morels and shiitake mushrooms by 10 to 20 percent.

I use a very small amount of powdered smoked pasilla chile for a slight smoky taste to the soup. If you can't find the pasilla, consider adding ¼ teaspoon or more of chipotle Tabasco.

Morel mushrooms sit on the chopping board awaiting their starring role in the pan. Photo by Andrew Schneider

Ingredients for 10 servings

Garlic, roasted	2 heads
Shallots, roasted	2 medium
Butter or olive oil	3 T
Sweet onion, minced	1 cup
Dried morel and/or porcini mushrooms	1½ oz.
White pepper	½ t
Thyme, dried	1 t
Sage, dried	1 T
Orange zest	1 t
Sea salt	2 t
Smoked Spanish paprika	½ t
Fresh wild mushrooms, cut in ⅓" strips	12 oz.
Beef, vegetable, or chicken broth	2 quarts (plus 4 cups for later)
Sherry, dry	½ cup
Brandy or Calvados	½ cup

Optional

Porcini bouillon cubes	2
Fennel, minced	½ cup
Smoked pasilla chile powder	½ t

Preheat the oven to 400 degrees. Cut top off garlic heads and shallots, drizzle with a little olive oil, wrap in foil, and bake for 45 minutes

Place the dried mushroom in a bowl, cover with 4 cups of hot broth, and soak for 30 minutes. I use the porcini bouillon cubes for extra flavor. Drain, reserve liquid, chop mushroom finely, and set aside.

In a heavy pot, melt butter or olive oil over medium heat, add onions (and the optional fennel), sauté about eight minutes, and stir occasionally until soft and lightly browned.

Stir in garlic and shallots.

Add drained and chopped dried mushrooms, stir, sauté for another two or three minutes, then add liquid from soaking. Add seasonings.

Add sliced fresh mushrooms, reserving a handful for garnish. Stir, add broth and bring to a light boil. Cover and cook for 20 minutes.

Remove from heat and use an in-pot blender or food processor to chop solids to the desired consistency.

Return to heat and add sherry, brandy, then reserved fresh mushrooms. Bring to a light boil, cover, and cook for 15 minutes.

Taste, adjust seasonings, and serve.

Oregon Scallop Confetti Soup

It really was a dark and stormy night. I drove across country: Washington, D.C., to Portland, Oregon. The first 2,800 miles were a breeze. The last 200 were stark terror.

Oregonians, dedicated to protecting all things natural, apparently don't believe in putting anything on the inches of glaze ice that collect on their roads, especially along the awesome stretch of weather proving-ground called the Columbia Gorge.

I survived the ice only to encounter what the local residents claimed was the worst windstorm in two decades. Electric power disappeared for three days. So there I was, overlooking the Columbia River in my overpriced yuppie apartment with its yuppie electric range.

Fearing the meat and fish I'd just bought would spoil, I stuck it all in a cooler filled with ice. And that's how this recipe started.

Ingredients for 8 servings

Fresh sea scallops	1 pound
Carrots, diced or sliced	3 oz.
Green onions, sliced thin	4
Red pepper, chopped	4 oz.
White mushrooms, sliced	4 large
Ginger root, thin slices	6
Chicken broth	8 cups
Sherry, dry	1 cup
Maggi	1 oz
Zest of lemon, lime, or orange	2 T
Salt and white pepper	

Take the fresh sea scallops and freeze slightly so they can be cut into thin strips without destroying the delicate meat.

Meanwhile, cut the carrots, green onions, and red peppers into small slices or julienne into strips. Thinly slice white button mushrooms.

Peel the ginger root and slice to about the thickness of a nickel.

Over medium heat (it can also be done over a camp stove) add chicken or vegetable broth, sherry, and ginger root to a saucepan. Bring to a boil. Add Maggi; simmer at just below a boil. Cover and cook for 10 minutes.

Add peppers, carrots, mushroom, and whites of green onion to the broth. Return to simmer and cook for two minutes. Add salt and white pepper to taste.

Add scallops, return to simmer and cook for one minute. Add zest of lemon, orange, or lime.

Serve in individual bowls and top with a few tips of green onions.

If the power is still out, light enough candles to see the attractive color combination of the soup.

Washington State — D.B. Cooper's Salmon Hash

Back in 1971, some guy that the world media and FBI named D.B. Cooper jumped out of a perfectly good Boeing 727 in the stormy night sky somewhere over Ariel, Washington.

A rotted bundle of about $15,800 was found years later on the bank of the Columbia River. The feds said the serial numbers matched some of the $200,000 that Cooper received when he hijacked the plane and its crew.

Every year, around Nov. 24, Cooper fans and treasure hunters gather in Ariel to party, swap lies and argue about what happened to the missing paratrooper.

This salmon hash is an adaptation of one served at a D.B. Cooper gathering.

Left: Wild king salmon on display at Pike Place Market in Seattle. Photo by Andrew Schneider

Ingredients for four servings

Smoked bacon	10 slices
Redskin potatoes	12 small
Red onion, sliced	1 large
Chopped fennel bulb	½ cup
Rye seed	¼ t
Fennel seeds	1 t
Celery seed	¼ t
Green pepper, cubed	½ cup
Red pepper, cubed	½ cup
Garlic, shaved	2 cloves
Alder-smoked salmon, flaked or sliced thin	1 lb.
Fresh dill, chopped	1 T
Sliced chanterelles	1½ cups
Olive oil	2 T
Kosher salt and pepper	

Slowly cook the bacon until crisp. Drain and save the grease.

Cut the potatoes, onions and fennel into cubes and toss with bacon grease. Add rye, fennel seed, and celery seed; bake in a flat pan for 30 minutes or until cooked through.

In a heavy skillet, heat olive oil and sauté cubed red and green pepper, chanterelles and shaved garlic. Stir and cook until just soft.

Add salmon, bacon, potatoes, onion, and fennel; stir gently.

Add chopped fresh dill, adjust seasonings, and serve with poached or basted eggs.

Washington State
Doctor Daughter's Poached Salmon

This recipe is from a tugboat pilot on the Columbia River who insists his name is Jimmy J. James, even though he has "Arthur" stitched on his windbreaker and is wearing a large, rusty belt buckle proclaiming "Big Bob."

While the old river rat may dance around his name, he's crystal clear about his distaste for poached fish.

"The only water that should be around a fish when it's being cooked is the little bit in the Scotch that the cook's drinking," he says.

He has had "a couple or so" heart attacks and his daughter, "the doctor," somehow got JJJ to promise to never eat fried food or red meat again.

So when Dr. Daughter comes out to the tug for her monthly visit, he says he "hides the good stuff and ruins a perfectly good hunk of fish by boiling it senseless."

Triple J is being unkind to his daughter's recipe. It tastes good and he knows it. This is an adaptation.

Ingredients for four servings

Carrots, sliced thin	½ cup
Celery, sliced thin	½ cup
Green onions, sliced thin	⅓ cup
Dry white vermouth	⅔ cups
Chicken stock	1½ cups
Lemon slices	6
Dijon mustard	1 T
Dill, dried	½ t
Thyme, dried	1 t
Sea salt	¼ t
White Pepper	¼ t
Salmon steaks, 1" thick	1½ lbs.

Into a saucepan, add vegetables, seasoning, vermouth, stock, lemon slices, and mustard.

"I throw in whatever green stuff I've got on the spice shelf," Triple J says. Dried dill and thyme work well, but fresh would be better. Season with sea salt and white pepper.

Heat ingredients to a boil, cover, and lower heat immediately. Simmer for 3 minutes.

Wash salmon in cold water, pat dry, and place in a glass baking dish. Pour hot mustard and lemon mixture over fish, cover tightly with foil, and place in a preheated 450-degree oven for 14 minutes for 1-inch-thick steak. Vary time for other thicknesses.

Remove from the oven and serve immediately.

If you want your salmon slightly drier, remove the foil during the last five minutes. If the seasoning that Doctor Daughter recommends isn't enough for you, brush fish with a bit of extra virgin olive oil, a few shavings of garlic and a touch of soy or Maggi sauce.

PRESS

THE OPERATOR OF THIS CAR IS

VII

Far and Wide

1961-2010

Far and Wide

Andy proposed to me at Reflection Lake on Mount Rainier. Then came the hard part: Where to get married? We had friends on both coasts and family in the East and Midwest. Someone was going to be inconvenienced no matter where we chose. So we opted to elope.

As an Army photographer and as a reporter, Andy had been everywhere: Europe, Asia, South America, Australia, New Zealand—even Antarctica. So I suggested Homer, Alaska, the "end of the road," because I loved the symbolism. But when I checked the prices, it was cheaper to fly to Europe.

Andy had been charmed by Beirut in his reporting travels. But parts of the beautiful city he had fallen for had fallen into ruin during Lebanon's civil war.

Above: Schneider leans against an ancient wall in Sicily checking his camera, in 2006. Photo by Kathy Best

We settled on Italy, which he had been to but never with time to play. A former colleague at the *Pittsburgh Press*, a well-connected religion writer, hooked us up with the Methodist missionary of Milan and we exchanged vows in his tiny chapel. The Korean workers making kimchi in the parish kitchen were our witnesses.

It was early October, the height of white truffle season. And Andy had done his homework. After a quick honeymoon in a Piedmont vineyard inn, we hit the road. We went truffle hunting with a former Italian champion named Paolo and his ace truffle-sniffing dog, shopped for truffles in Alba and interviewed the chef of a restaurant in Gubbio who created an all-truffle fall menu that drew diners from Rome. Andy, of course, wrote about all of it when we returned to Seattle.

Andy pets the former Italian champion truffle-hunting dog during our 1998 honeymoon in Italy. Photo by Kathy Best

I didn't think anything could top that Italian adventure until the Cutraro family, friends we met in St. Louis, invited us to join them when the patriarch of the family returned to Sicily for the first time in more than two decades. We were treated—and ate—like royalty as various Cutraro cousins vied to outdo each other. One meal on a hilltop farm with glimpses of the Mediterranean began at 11 a.m. and was still going at 8 that night.

Out exploring another day, Andy and I peeled off and drove through the hot, arid center of Sicily on our own. We stopped at a restaurant where the only other customer was a man in his 80s. He heard Andy talking and asked in halting English if he was American, then told us he had been saved by the Americans after hiding from the Germans in World War II. He asked the cook to bring Andy a dish that turned out to be pasta carbonara. The man's grin grew with every bite Andy took. "The best! The best!" he proclaimed as he thumped his chest. He was so right.

I'm still not quite sure how Andy made it to New Zealand, although it could have been a stop en route to Antarctica to take pictures for the Army. Whatever the reason, it paid off when I took him home to Illinois for Easter, where my family always ate leg of lamb for the holiday. My dad, the lamb cook, had died the year before, and Mom had announced to Andy that he would be cooking. In a slight panic, he reached out to a guy he'd met in Christchurch—Andy suspected he was a spy for the Brits—and got a recipe. Spy or not, the Kiwi knew how to cook lamb.

Far and Wide

Italy
Essence of Italy Soup
Great Italian Grain Salad
It's Really Not Italian Wedding Soup
Pasta Carbonara with Pancetta and Prosciutto

Japan
Dried and Fresh Shiitake Cure-All Soup

Lebanon
Beirut Lentil Soup

New Zealand
Christ Church Leg of Lamb
Lamb Shanks of a Suspected Spy

Italy — Essence of Italy Soup

This hearty soup, great for enduring foul weather, blends the best of Italy's most popular vegetables, herbs, cured meats, cheese and grain. I adapted this recipe from versions of the soup we enjoyed in Sicily and in an inn near Naples.

The grandmother of a friend told me that a money-saving trick many Italian cooks use when the flavor of prosciutto or Parmigiano-Reggiano is needed is to get your butcher to sell you the less expensive, left-over ends of the smoked meat and the cheesemonger to give you the rind from the cheese.

In making this soup, you can shave the cheese off the rind and toss the remainder into the soup. I usually remove the cooked rind before serving because it's very chewy, but others chop it into very small pieces, which some really enjoy.

If fresh porcini mushrooms are available, slice thin and sauté in olive oil or butter over a medium heat for about two minutes.

Farro, which culinary historians say goes back to the Roman legions, is called by many in the Mediterranean "the mother of all wheat." Some consider it a bit tricky to cook, but its great nutty flavor is worth the effort. Carefully read instruction on the farro. Some have to be soaked in water overnight. Others can be used immediately. Also consider other grains. I have had this soup with barley and even short-grain rice.

Left: Porcini mushrooms, a Schneider favorite, await brushing before being added to a soup. Photo by Andrew Schneider

Ingredients for 12 servings

Olive oil, extra virgin	3 T
Prosciutto, ¼" thick, trimmed well and cut in ½" pieces	8 oz.
Onion, red or sweet, chopped fine	1 large
Celery and leaves, sliced thin	1 cup
Carrots, sliced thin	1 cup
Garlic, minced	4 cloves
Chicken, vegetable, or mushroom stock, rich	12 cups
Parmigiano-Reggiano cheese rind, cut in 2" squares	3 pieces
Italian farro	1½ cups
Porcini mushroom, dried	½ cup
Sun-dried tomatoes in oil,	¼ cup or chopped
or diced fresh tomatoes,	1 cup
Basil, fresh, slice into thin strips	3 bunches (about 4 oz.)
Parmigiano-Reggiano, shaved and set aside	2 oz.
Fennel, chopped fine (save fronds for garnish)	⅔ cups
Oregano, fresh, chopped fine	3 T (or 1½ T dried)
Sage, fresh, chopped fine	2 T (or 1 T dried)
Sea salt and coarse black pepper to taste	

Heat olive oil in a heavy-bottomed soup pot over medium heat. Add prosciutto, including a bit of the fat to enhance flavor. Cook for 2 minutes, then add onions and stir. Cook until onions are soft and meat is browned. Add celery, carrots, fennel, and garlic during the last minute or so. Stir.

Add stock to the pot. Toss in cheese rind and farro and bring to boil; then reduce to light boil.

Add mushrooms and sun-dried tomatoes with olive oil drained off. If using diced canned or fresh tomatoes, add juice you can save.

Add basil leaves to soup. Stir. Add curls or pieces of Parmigiano-Reggiano, oregano, and sage. Remember that the cheese and the cured meat are both salty so add sea salt and coarse black pepper carefully, to taste. Cook for 30 minutes or until farro is tender.

Italy Great Italian Grain Salad

I've had this salad made with different grains but I think that farro—an ancient, nutty Italian grain—is the best by far. Culinary historians say farro—loaded with nutrients—fed the Roman army and its firm, chewy texture presents a versatile canvas for broad ranges of flavors.

There is lots of confusion over identifying and naming farro. When I first saw it used in Gubbio, a hill town in Umbria, an English-speaking cook in the kitchen said it was spelt wheat. But a visiting cook standing nearby said spelt wheat is called farro in Italian but hastened to add, some call it emmer. Of course, you can go for the classic Latin and ask for *Triticum dicoccum.*

Something to watch out for: Some farro, depending on where it was cultivated, has to be soaked for at least eight hours before cooking. Cracked farro, which I use in this recipe, can be rinsed, checked for impurities and cooked straight out without soaking.

Adapted from a recipe from Ristorante Pizzeria All'Antico Frantoio in Gubbio, Italy.

Left: Great Italian Grain Salad. Photo by Vincent J. Musi

Ingredients for 10 servings

Hazelnuts, chopped coarsely	⅓ cup
Porcini bouillon	1 cube
(or 1 oz. reconstituted dried mushrooms)	
Chicken, vegetable, or beef broth	6 cups
Shallot, minced	¼ cup
Garlic, minced	3 cloves
Olive oil	3 T
Italian farro	2 cups
Maggi seasoning	1 T
Grape tomatoes, halved	1 cup
Green onion, sliced ⅓" wide	⅔ cup
Capers	2 T
Artichokes hearts, quartered	½ cup
Peppers, red, green or yellow sweet sliced into ½" pieces	½ cup

Dressing

Lime juice	3 T
Lime zest	1½ t
Sherry vinegar	2 T
Olive oil, extra virgin	⅓ cup
Garlic, minced	2 cloves
Sea salt and pepper to taste	

Preheat the oven to 350 degrees.

Place coarsely chopped nuts on foil and roast for 4½ minutes.

Place bouillon cube or dried mushrooms in 1 cup hot broth.

To make the farro, chop shallots and garlic, then sauté until softened in three tablespoons of olive oil in a heavy saucepan.

Add farro to the pan, stirring well. Add broth, porcini bouillon cube or reconstituted dried mushrooms, Maggi sauce, and broth. Stir.

Bring to boil and reduce heat to medium, cooking uncovered for 30-45 minutes or until liquid is absorbed. Set aside.

When grain is cooled, add tomatoes, green onions, capers, artichoke hearts, sweet peppers, and toasted nuts. Add dressing. Stir gently but well and serve either chilled or at room temperature.

Italy It's Really Not Italian Wedding Soup

I came across this recipe when we were honeymooning in Gubbio, but I learned that the popular soup has nothing to do with matrimony. It is just a perfect blend of any two ingredients. In this case, a wonderful, rich broth and marble-sized balls of pork, beef or poultry. My valued friend Vince Musi explains "this marriage of ingredients—greens and meat—is called Minestra Maritata."

When we were served this in Gubbio, the pasta was acini di pepe, but any tiny noodle will do. Often I use the rice-shaped orzo.

Ingredients for 10 servings (as a first course)

or four (as a main course)

Olive oil, extra virgin	3 T
Garlic, chunked	2 large cloves
Garlic, minced	2 cloves
Shallots, peeled and minced	2 T
Celery, sliced	1 cup
Carrots, julienned	1 cup
Onion, sweet	½ cup
Shiitake or porcini mushrooms, fresh, thick sliced	½ lb.
Chicken stock, rich	10 cups
Orzo or other tiny pasta	1 cup
Baby spinach leaves sliced ⅓" thick	4 cups
or Escarole, coarsely chopped	4 cups
Grape tomatoes	10
Basil leaves, fresh, sliced ⅓" thick	¼ cup
Sea salt	½ t
White pepper	¼ t
Meatballs: Ground turkey, pork or beef, ground	16 oz.
Egg, well beaten	1, large
Panko breadcrumbs	⅓ cup
Garlic, chopped fine	2 large or 4 medium cloves
Shallots, chopped fine	¼ cup
Basil, fresh, chopped	2 T
Parsley, chopped	2 T
Nutmeg	½ t
Salt and pepper to taste	

For serving

Parmigiano Reggiano cheese, grated

For the meatballs

Preheat the oven to 350 degrees.

In a medium bowl, add ingredients for meatballs and form into balls about ¾ inches in diameter. Set on a foil-lined, oiled baking pan and cook for 12–15 minutes depending on size. Check for doneness early. Remove the meatballs from the pan and, after draining briefly on a paper towel, add to the simmering soup.

For the soup

Heat the olive oil in a heavy soup pot. Add garlic chunks and cook until browned. Remove garlic from oil and discard.

Lower heat to medium. Add shallots, minced garlic, celery, carrots and onions. Stir and cook for 3 or 4 minutes until soft. Add mushrooms and cook for another 3 minutes.

Add broth and bring to a slow boil. Cover, reduce heat, and simmer for 20 minutes. Add pasta and simmer for 10 more minutes.

Add spinach or escarole, basil, grape tomatoes, and meatballs.

Salt and pepper to taste.

Bring to a boil and serve immediately.

Above right: Pasta Carbonara. Photo by Terry Dragotta

Italy Pasta Carbonara with Prosciutto

After exploring the coast of Sicily, we decided one day to head across the center of the island. The menu of the restaurant in the small hotel atop a cliff overlooking the arid valley of Agira listed an impressive offering of Sicilian dishes.

This recipe was recommended by an old man who recognized my American accent and wanted to tell me, in very broken English and much chest thumping, the story of how the Americans had saved him. He said this dish was the best. And he was right.

While carbonara is a favorite pasta for many, some avoid it because of concerns about what the cream and excessive butter will do to calorie counting and cholesterol. This recipe offers almost the same richness because of the use of additional coarsely ground hard cheese. So reducing the amount of butter and substituting milk for heavy cream works well.

Have your butcher slice the prosciutto about one-quarter to one-third of an inch thick. Or use pancetta, an Italian bacon cured with salt, pepper and other spices, but not smoked. In a pinch, regular thick-sliced bacon can be used. Parmigiano Reggiano cheese or pecorino Romano work well. But so will an American cheese called Vella's dry jack, which was used as a substitute for Parmesan during World War II when cheese wasn't imported from Italy.

Ingredients for six servings

Bacon, thick sliced	2 slices
Prosciutto or pancetta, cut into ¼" cubes	6 oz.
Butter, unsalted	4 T
Capers	1½ T
Milk or cream	1 cup
Parmigiano Reggiano cheese, grated coarsely	1½ cups
Salt and pepper to taste	
Fettuccine or linguine	16 oz.
Eggs, beaten vigorously	2 large

In a sauté pan large enough to hold the al dente pasta, slowly cook the bacon over a medium heat until crisp. Remove the bacon, add the prosciutto, and lower the heat.

Add the butter and capers; stir.

Add milk and cheese; stir.

Add salt and pepper as needed. Be careful if you're using salted capers; little salt may be needed.

Break cooked bacon into small pieces; add and stir.

Cook pasta al dente, as Sicilians prefer. Drain well, reserving some pasta water, and add to the sauté pan.

Quickly add well-beaten eggs and blend well. If too dry, add a bit of pasta water to achieve creamy consistency.

Japan Shiitake Cure-All soup

This was adapted from a recipe for a soup that I was served three times a day for almost a week in Yokosuka, Japan, where I was sick as a dog while taking a break from shooting photos in Vietnam.

Initially, this soup was served to me as a fish broth, but I think it's much tastier in a chicken or pork stock.

Ingredients for 4 servings

Shiitake mushrooms, fresh or dried	4 oz.
Garlic, minced	2 cloves
Ginger, grated	1 T
Sake or mirin	2 T
Tamari or soy sauce	4 T
Rice vinegar	1 T
Spinach, coarsely chopped	1 cup
Chicken or pork broth	8 cups
Green or spring onions, finely chopped	4
Soba (buckwheat) noodles	8 oz.

If using dried mushrooms, soak for 20 minutes. Add fresh or soaked mushrooms to the broth with minced garlic and ginger.

Bring to a boil. Reduce heat to medium and simmer for 10 minutes. Add sake or mirin, soy sauce or tamari, and rice vinegar.

Clean spinach and chop coarsely. Add to the pot with hot broth and cook over low heat for 5 minutes. Cut spring or green onions and cook for 4 minutes.

Boil soba, drain and divide among 4 soup bowls, Ladle the soup over the top.

Beirut Lentil Soup. Photo by Pamela Baker-Masson

Lebanon — Beirut Lentil Soup

Touring a neighborhood market in Beirut with some very patient friends was a circus of colors and aromas. They showed me drums of spices and bins filled with a dozen different shades of red, green and brown lentils, a staple in Middle Eastern and Indian kitchens. As the colors vary, so does the cooking time and ultimate texture or firmness of each. But the difference in taste is subtle.

The brown lentil is most commonly used worldwide and can range from a sandy tan to black in color. I learned during my tour that the darker the color, the more earthy and rich the flavor will be. Green lentils, also called *Lentilles du Puy*, are very popular in France and Italy and often used in cold salads because they hold their shape well. The red lentil, also called *masoor*, is most often used for soups and casseroles.

The thickness of the soup varies by personal taste and can easily be adjusted by adding more or less broth. I've found that paprika is a key seasoning, and smoked Spanish or Hungarian paprika works well. I didn't believe it at first, but my Lebanese friend's Uncle Tommas was correct: carefully selected canned tomatoes offered consistently better flavor than the cardboard-tasting fresh tomatoes usually sold in grocery stores.

Ingredients for 10 single-cup servings

Olive oil, extra virgin	4 T
Carrots, sliced thin or diced	1 cup
Onion and/or sliced fennel, finely cut	½ cup
Celery, sliced thin	½ cup
Plum tomatoes, canned diced tomatoes with sauce	1 lb. fresh or 14 oz.
Garlic, minced	3 cloves
Cumin, ground	2 heaping t
Coriander, ground	1 heaping t
Cinnamon, ground	½ heaping t
Smoked paprika	1 heaping t
Red lentils, washed and drained	2 cups
Chicken, vegetable, or mushroom stock	8 cups
Lemon zest	1 T
Lemon juice	3 T
Sea salt	1 t
Black pepper	½ t

Optional

Pancetta, thick bacon or chorizo	6 oz.
Parmigiano Reggiano cheese, grated	⅓ cup
Paprika-coated sea salt flakes	1 T

Dice carrots, celery and onion to same small size.

In a soup pot, cook bacon, pancetta or chorizo over medium heat until browned. Remove the meat from the pot and set aside.

Add 1 T olive oil to drippings, then add carrots, celery and onion and/or sliced fennel; cook on medium heat about 5 minutes or until soft.

Cut tomatoes in quarters or smaller pieces, then add to the pot. Stir and add the garlic, cumin, coriander, cinnamon, and smoked paprika.

Add red lentils. Stir and cook for 3 minutes. Add broth, lemon zest. Bring to a light boil. Add cooked meat, lower heat, cover, and simmer for 10 minutes, stirring frequently. Remove lid and simmer another 10 minutes.

Add lemon juice, salt and pepper to taste and adjust other seasonings. Cook until the lentils and carrots are tender.

Garnish with a few drops of quality olive oil or a thin twist of lemon skin. Finish with a light sprinkle of paprika-coated sea salt flakes.

New Zealand — Christ Church Leg of Lamb

I adapted this recipe from Friar Mikhail or Michael. It changed each of the times I met him. He said he was an Anglican friar, but I think he was a spy—not that the two career paths are mutually exclusive.

I met him in Cambodia during the Vietnam War and then on the Thai border with Laos. Three years later I stumbled across him again in a tiny town just a bit south of Christchurch, New Zealand. He said he was studying the faith healing of the Maori religion.

To support my belief that the good friar was a spy, he used a spice blend he said he learned about from the Republic of Georgia. It had a base of coarse kosher or sea salt and a bit of caraway, coriander, black pepper, garlic and some smoky chile powder. To my pleasant surprise, I found that a Seattle spice monger, World Spice Merchant, sold something very similar called Svaneti Salt.

Regardless of his true profession, Friar Mikhail was obsessed with lamb. He said he loved New Zealand because sheep outnumber people by 15 to 1. He shared two recipes with me, leg of lamb and lamb shanks. I dug out his recipe for leg of lamb when I got drafted to cook the traditional Easter feast for Kathy's family.

Ingredients for 8 servings

Leg of lamb	8 lbs.
Garlic	6 cloves
or pearl onions	8 small

For rub

Kosher salt	1¼ t
Green or black peppercorns	1 t
Rosemary, dried	1 t

Marinade

Kosher salt	½ t
Peppercorns	½ t
Rosemary, dried	1 t
Garlic	2 cloves
Mustard, Dijon-style	2 T
Maggi seasoning or light soy sauce	2 T
Dark rum	2 T
Olive oil, extra virgin	¼ cup
Red wine	2 T
Honey or brown sugar	1 T

Mix ingredients for marinade.

Trim excess fat off the leg, leaving a thin layer.

Crush salt, peppercorns, and rosemary together; rub well into lamb.

Cut ½-inch slices into the lamb and insert a clove of garlic or half a pearl onion.

Place lamb in a large Ziploc bag, add marinade, force out extra air, seal, and refrigerate for 2 hours to overnight, depending on how intense you want the flavoring.

Preheat oven to 500 degrees

Place the lamb on a greased rack, fat side up.

Roast for 10 minutes at 500 degrees, then lower to 350 degrees and cook about 20 minutes a pound or until internal temperature reaches 145 degrees, which is medium and pink inside.

Allow the roast to rest for 10 minutes before carving.

To carve, insert a fork into the wide end of the roast, cut thin slices, perpendicular to the bone, then run the knife along the bone to free the slices. Remove slices to a platter and serve.

New Zealand Shanks of a Suspected Spy

Friar Mikhail had recipes for every cut of lamb. If a leg is too big for your appetite, try his shanks.

Above: Shanks of a Suspected Spy. Photo by Paul Kitagaki Jr.

Ingredients for 6 servings

Lamb shanks, either whole or split	6 large
Flour	½ cup
Olive oil	⅓ cup
Svaneti seasoning or salt and pepper, ground	1 T
Mushrooms, halved	¾ lb.
Sweet onions, coarsely chopped	1½ cups
Brussels sprouts, halved	1½ cups
Carrots, chopped ½" pieces	2 cups
Garlic, peeled and chopped coarsely	12 cloves
Tomatoes, diced fresh or good quality canned	2 cups
Prunes or currants	1 cup
Sage leaves	2 T
Rosemary	4 T
White pepper	½ t
Kosher salt	1 T
Nutmeg	1 t
Beef or chicken stock	8 cups

1 bottle of full-bodied red wine, preferably Bordeaux

Trim excess fat from the shanks.

Over medium high flame, heat oil in heavy pot, enameled cast iron, if you have one.

Dredge lamb shanks in flour seasoned with salt and pepper or Svaneti seasoning, if you can find it. Shake off excess. Add shanks to oil and cook over medium high heat, turning until well-browned on all sides.

Remove from pot.

Add onions and carrots to the oil and cook for four or five minutes, stirring well.

Add garlic, cooking one minute. Add mushrooms, Brussels sprouts and tomato. Cook 2 minutes and stir.

Add prunes or currants, chopped sage and rosemary

Add stock to cover shanks, wine and seasonings. Cover, bring to a boil, lower heat to a simmer and cook 2½ hours or until lamb is tender. If cooking on stovetop, turn shanks every 30 minutes.

If sauce is too thin, remove meat and vegetables, set aside and increase heat on pot and reduce sauce until it will stick to the back of a metal spoon.

1967

Caribbean International News Service

VISITOR A 0864

Southern Correspondents Reporting Racial Equality Wars

UNITED STATES OF AMERICA
DEPARTMENT OF DEFENSE
WASHINGTON 25, D.C.

NONCOMBATANT'S CERTIFICATE OF IDENTITY

N120546

PROPERTY OF U.S. GOVERNMENT

WORK PHOTO
ANDREW
of the UNITE

ORGANIZATION OF AMERICAN STATES

PRESIDENTIAL

Andrew Schneider
Name

signature OAS

OFFICIAL PRESS
ANDREW SCHNEIDER
C.I.N.S.
NASSAU

Issued By
St. Augustine Police Dept.

CINCLANT
SUB JIB SANTO DOMINGO

NAME
THE ABOVE NAMED PERSON HAS
REGISTERED WITH THE SUB JIB
SANTO DOMINGO COURTESIES AND
ASSISTANCE WILL BE RENDERED

PRESS PASS

VIII

At Home and Family

1959-2017

Schneider uses the in-pot blender on a soup in his Chesapeake Bay kitchen in 2006. Photo by Andrew Cutraro

At Home and Family

Food was a throughline in Andy's family, as well as in his life.

His great-grandmother—his Bubbe—owned restaurants in Brooklyn and Connecticut and taught him to cook latkes, render *schmaltz* and make chopped liver.

His father, an immigrant from Hungary, went to culinary school when he got out of the Army and passed on his recipe for Hungarian soups. Jack Schneider also worked as the maitre d' at the Fountainbleu Hotel on Miami Beach, making tableside Caesar salads. That recipe was passed down through the male line to Andy, son Patrick and Patrick's sons, Quinn and Ethan, following the family tradition.

Schneider with son Patrick and grandsons Ethan, left, and Quinn hold the ingredients for the family Caesar salad recipe in the bowl Andy's father used as a maitre d'. Photo by Kathy Best

Kelly, Andy's very independent daughter, and I altered that way-too-patrilineal tradition and snagged the recipe for ourselves since we both loved Caesar salad. As a single mom, Kelly doesn't have much time to cook for fun. But she loves good food and is making sure her daughter, Josie, knows her way around the kitchen.

I was usually Andy's sous chef, which translated into cutting, fetching, and stirring dishes that required long attention at the stove. I also handled anything that involved a crust or required precise measurements.

Schneider and Best prepare a dinner of smoked salmon in Des Moines, Washington. Photo by Paul Kitagaki Jr.

While cakes, cookies and pies weren't Andy's thing, candy was. Especially the peanut brittle made by our Post-Dispatch colleague Mandy St. Amand. When we left St. Louis and headed back to Seattle, we adapted her recipe, using hazelnuts instead of peanuts. Try it; it's divine.

Grandson Ethan is still at the Naval Academy as I write this. Quinn has graduated from Annapolis and, at last report, is cooking up a storm in Pensacola when he's not learning to fly the Navy's planes. I hope both get the chance to eat their way around the world, logging adventures at every stop.

At Home and Family

Soups
Hungarian Cauliflower Soup

Sides
Bubbe's Latkes
Good Morning Biscuits and Sausage Gravy
Fried Green Tomatoes
Southern Surprise Cornbread Dressing
Walla Walla Sweet Onion Pie
"What am I, chopped liver?"

Sweets
Patrick's Cranberry Experiment
Holiday Hazelnut Brittle

Soups Hungarian Cauliflower Soup

My mother and father rarely fought and, if they did, it was never in the kitchen. However, I do remember one exception: this cauliflower soup. My father, who was the family's trained cook and first-generation Hungarian, wanted the broth heavy with tender florets and enough paprika to give the soup a bright red color. My mom favored the liberal use of yellow curry and for the soup to be blended creamy smooth. Following is my peacekeeping compromise.

Ingredients for 8 servings

Cauliflower florets	2½ lbs.
Leek, thinly sliced	1
Butter	4 T
Olive oil	2 T
Sweet onion, finely chopped	1 large
Celery, thinly sliced	1 cup
Garlic, crushed	3 cloves
Sweet Hungarian paprika	1 T
Curry powder	¾ T
Chicken or vegetable stock	8 cups
Thyme	1 t
White pepper, coarse	½ t
Sea salt	1 t

Optional

Pancetta, finely diced	6 slices
Breadcrumbs with white truffle oil	½ cup

Remove florets from the core of two large cauliflowers, cut large pieces in half, rinse well, and set aside.

Thinly slice leek lengthwise and rinse well under cold water to remove sand.

Melt butter and olive oil in heavy large pot over medium heat. Add garlic, onion, sliced celery, and leek. Sauté until tender, about 8 minutes.

Add cauliflower and sauté another 5 minutes.

Add stock and seasonings. Cover and simmer until cauliflower is tender, about 25 minutes.

Remove about one cup of cauliflower florets and set aside.

Using an in-pot blender, puree the remainder of the soup to desired consistency.

Return the cup of cooked cauliflower to pot.

Return soup to pot. (Soup can be prepared a day ahead. Cool slightly. Cover and refrigerate.) Bring soup to simmer.

Season to taste with salt and pepper.

Garnish with pieces of crispy pancetta or, just before serving, dust each bowl of soup with about 2 teaspoons of well-toasted bread sprinkled with white truffle oil ground into breadcrumbs.

"The last time I tasted Hungarian Cauliflower Soup was in Andy's kitchen in Seattle, and my first sip of my finished product took me back there instantly." Testing and photo by David McCumber

Sides Bubbe's Latkes

The battle over how potato pancakes or latkes should be made has been fought in home kitchens and delis for generations. It is almost always focused on the crispness of the eastern European delicacy. If it's not crispy, don't call it a latke.

My great grandmother would sometimes use grated carrots and onions in place of potatoes. She even produced the wonderful side dish with kasha or buckwheat groats.

For the best latkes, cook with schmaltz. It has a higher smoke point, better taste and can be found at most better markets if you don't make your own.

One secret upon which most experienced cooks agree: Always make more than you think they'll eat.

Ingredients for 20 servings

Russet potatoes, shredded	3 lbs.
Sweet onion, chopped small	2 cups
Eggs	3 large
Matzo meal	⅓ cup
Coarse salt	1 T
Black pepper	½ T
Schmaltz (chicken or duck fat)	⅔ cup

Left: Bubbe's latkes. Photo by Vincent J. Musi

Preheat the oven to 200 degrees. Line a baking pan with paper towels and place rack on top. Set aside.

Use either the grating blade on a food processor or the large hole side of a four-sided grater, grate the potatoes and onions into a bowl. (The food processor is faster and much easier.) Place the mixture into a strainer or a clean cotton dishtowel and squeeze out as much liquid as possible. The more you remove, the crisper the pancakes will be.

Mix the eggs in another bowl, adding matzo meal, salt, pepper. Then add potatoes and onions, mixing well.

Melt ⅓ cup of schmaltz in skillet until it sizzles.

Place a full tablespoon of the potato onion mixture into the hot oil and flatten with the back of a spoon. Cook 3 to 5 minutes on each side until browned.

Replenish schmaltz after each batch is cooked to keep ⅓ inch in pan. Note that the pan will get hotter over time, so adjust heat as needed so you don't burn the latkes.

As latkes come out of the pan, sprinkle with salt, place on the rack and put pan inside the warm oven.

Serve with applesauce, apple butter or sour cream.

Sides Good Morning Biscuits and Sausage Gravy

The South did rise again, and this recipe is the reason why.

This is an adaptation of an almost century-old recipe I was taught as a child by a wonderful woman named Carrie. All I remember was that she would always say, "The biscuits must be wonderful and oh so light. Sausage so tasty that it brings tears."

Ingredients for 4 servings

Biscuits

Self-rising flour	2 cups
Baking powder	2½ t
Salt	¾ t
Unsalted butter, cold, cut into chips	6 T
Milk	¾ cup

Mix butter with flour with a light, quick touch. Add milk, stirring quickly. Knead out on a flat surface. Roll out and cut dough in circles.

Place on baking sheet and bake at 425 degrees in a preheated oven for 10 to 15 minutes.

Gravy

Pork sausage	1 lb.
Flour	3 T
Milk	2 cups
Half and half	1 cup
Kosher salt	½ t
Coarse black pepper	1 t
Old Bay seasoning	½ t
Tabasco	a dash

While biscuits are cooking, crumble sausage in hot pan and cook over medium heat until there is no pink.

Add flour one tablespoon at a time. Stir quickly until all the sausage is coated.

Add milk and half-and-half, one cup at a time, and stir until mixture thickens.

Add salt and pepper to taste.

Sides Fried Green Tomatoes

In the 1980s, recipes for fried green tomatoes would send the health conscious screaming from the kitchen. But those who appreciate deep, rich, true flavors would be racing for the stove.

This recipe is adapted from my childhood, when they were cooked by Carrie, the wonderful, ageless woman who would fight with my father over food and get away with it. Carrie, who often showed up with a brown sack of goodies from her garden, said she was the great-great-granddaughter of a plantation cook. (I don't know if her ancestor was enslaved and she didn't talk about it.)

She said she was taught that to serve green tomatoes without a gravy was a sin that would burn you in hell. All I can really remember was that she fried the tomatoes in lard. To whatever grease that was left after the tomatoes were cooked, she added a bit of milk or cream, maybe a half cup or so, and a little flour and salt and pepper and mixed it well. She then poured the thickened gravy over the tomatoes and served.

As a concession to my father, I think I remember her occasionally also dredging the tomatoes in flour, but only when my father was looking, which he made me believe he never did.

Over the years, I have seen tomatoes dredged in everything from stone-cut coarse white grits to fine rye bread crumbs to fine Italian polenta or cornmeal. The humble tomatoes have been adorned with everything from red sauce, blue cheese, sharp cheddar, pesto and Old Bay seasoning to slivers of country ham, grilled shrimp and even toasted marshmallow—and that's just in the southern U.S. In Canada, I once had them served with maple syrup and a bit of maple sugar.

If you want to try it Carrie's way, with gravy, I would omit the flour and cornmeal and just fry about 45 seconds on each side.

My concession to both Carrie and my father is that I cook these in bacon fat.

Ingredients for four servings

Kosher salt	to taste
Black pepper, coarse	to taste
Green tomatoes, fresh, firm, sliced ¼" thick	4, large
Fatback, side pork or thick smoked bacon, cut in 1" pieces	8 oz.
Eggs	2
Maggi seasoning	1 T
Flour	1 cup
Yellow cornmeal	1 cup

Salt and pepper sliced tomatoes and set aside.

Place bacon or fatback in a heavy, large skillet over medium heat. Cook until pork is crisp and removed and set aside. Retain fat in the skillet.

Lightly beat the eggs in a low bowl. Season with salt, pepper, and Maggi, and set aside.

Dredge the seasoned tomatoes in flour and shake off excess, then dip into egg mixture. Gently press into cornmeal and again shake off excess.

Lay in heated fat in skillet and cook over medium heat until browned, about 90 seconds. Turn and cook another 60-90 seconds or until other side is browned.

Drain on a paper towel. Keep warm in 200-degree oven until served.

Sides: Southern Surprise Cornbread Dressing

This is my recollection of the wonderful stuffing that I grew up with down South. It was made by Carrie, a generous, ageless woman who often cared for us while our parents worked two jobs. She called this Big Boss' Holiday Stuffing and said her great-grandmother, a cook for years on a Georgia cotton plantation, taught her the recipe. The surprise comes from fruit added to the savory mixture. Carrie used pieces of peach or plum. I often use the sweets of the Pacific Northwest like dried cherries, cranberries or apple.

While Carrie cooked the stuffing in the turkey, I cook it in a casserole dish because it's easy to ensure that it's properly cooked, and it is more crispy and caramelized in places.

Ingredients for eight servings

Pecan pieces, toasted	1½ cups
Cornbread	8 cups
Country sausage	1 lb.
Smoked bacon or fatback	4 oz.
Sweet butter or olive oil	½ cup
Mushrooms, sauteed	1 cup
Sweet onion, chopped	1½ cups
Celery, sliced thin	1½ cups
Dried tart cherries	1½ cups
Bourbon for soaking	
Garlic, minced	4 cloves
Cilantro or parsley, chopped	1 cup
Sage	3 T
Thyme	2 T
Salt and pepper to taste	
Eggs	3
Chicken broth, rich	3-4 cups

Put cherries into bowl and cover the bowl of cherries with bourbon, soaking at least 45 minutes.

Carefully toast the pecan pieces in a 300-degree oven until fragrant and slightly browned. Use caution to avoid burning because nuts can go from properly roasted to horribly charred very quickly.

Place cooked cornbread, homemade or store bought, on a baking pan or cookie sheet and leave on the counter overnight to dry out, or bake for an hour (or until dried) in a 250-degree oven. When cool, break into quarter-sized pieces.

Over medium heat, in a heavy, large skillet, cook sausage and fatback or bacon until browned, but not overcooked. Remove meat from the skillet but retain the fat. Add butter and melt, then add mushrooms, onions, and celery. Cook slowly until softened and slightly browned. Add garlic and seasonings and mix.

In a mixing bowl, gently blend meat, onions, and celery. Add cornbread pieces and 3 beaten eggs, tossing gently. Add toasted pecans, soaked dried cherries and cilantro or parsley. Add chicken broth. If too dry, add a bit more stock or apple cider. Be careful not to mix too vigorously so dressing doesn't become mushy.

Preheat oven to 350 degrees. Spoon dressing into a greased baking dish, spread evenly, and cover with foil. Bake for 40 to 45 minutes, removing foil after the first 15 minutes.

Locally grown Walla Walla sweet onions became a staple of Schneider's cooking in Washington state. Photo by Elana Winsberg

Sides Walla Walla Sweet Onion Pie

"Onion pie will cure a cold, fix a broken heart and remind you why life is good," or so said a fine old cook I met in Halfmoon Landing, Georgia, after a puny hurricane named Alberto flooded a good part of the state.

When we lived closer to Walla Walla than Vidalia, I substituted the equally delicious Washington onions for their Georgia cousins.

Ingredients for 12 servings

Maui, Vidalia, or Walla Walla onions, sliced thin	3 large
Thick smoked bacon	5 strips
Butter	3 oz.
Flour	1½ T
White pepper	½ t
Ginger, ground	¼ t
Nutmeg, ground	½ t
Milk, whole	1¼ cup
Vermouth, white	3 oz.
Eggs, large	3
Kosher salt	1 t
Pie-sized pastry shells	2
Fine cornmeal or flour	4 oz.

Preheat the oven to 375 degrees.

Thinly slice the onions.

Ribbon cut bacon into thin slices and cook until crisp in a large sauté pan. Add butter. Add the sliced onions and cook gently until softened and translucent. Add flour or cornmeal and spices and whisk in milk, stirring until thickened. Turn heat down to low, add vermouth, and cook one minute.

Remove from heat and let cool to near room temperature. Gently stir in beaten eggs.

Pour into two regular pie shells (makes 1.5" high pies) and let rest for five minutes.

Place in 375-degree oven for 25 minutes or until a knife stuck into the center comes out clean.

Sides "What Am I, Chopped Liver?"

I have friends and family members who flat out refuse to eat chopped liver of any kind—chicken, calf or beef. But if you call it paté or mousse, they'll scarf it down. Perhaps translating a couple of strange-sounding ingredients would help in increasing its palatability. For example, *schmaltz* is just chicken or duck fat. Think about the very tasty and popular duck confit. And then there's *grieven*, which is called cracklings throughout much of the world, and is just chicken skin cooked slowly until it's crisp.

This is my great-grandmother's recipe.

Ingredients for six servings

Eggs, hardboiled	2 large
Cracklings, minced very fine	2 T
Schmaltz (chicken or duck fat)	3 T
Sweet onion, sliced thin	4 cups
Garlic, minced	4 cloves
Chicken liver, washed and trimmed	1 lb.
Red onion, minced	4 T
Brandy or Calvados	1 T
Sea salt and fresh-ground pepper, to taste	

Left: Walla Walla onions at Pike Place Market.
Photo by Andrew Schneider

Hard boil eggs, peel and set aside.

Slowly sauté chicken skin over a low heat until crisp. Then drain on paper towels. Cut the 4 onions into ¼" slices.

Melt 4 tablespoons of chicken or duck fat into a large skillet over medium heat and add onion. Cook until softened, about 10 minutes.

Add garlic. Lower heat to lowest level, cover, and cook for another 30 minutes. Stir occasionally to avoid burning.

Wash liver and trim off anything you think you don't want to eat. Then add 1 tablespoon chicken or duck fat to another skillet and, over a medium heat, add the liver seasoned with salt and pepper. Cook until firm, lightly browned, and just slightly pink. Set aside and let cool.

Using a food processor with a metal blade, add liver, cooked sweet and raw red onions, cracklings, brandy, and hard-boiled eggs. Grind or chop livers until desired consistency is reached. I like it country-style, or coarse, or you can make it fine for the paté or mousse lovers.

Add salt and pepper to taste. If the liver is too dry, add another tablespoon of fat.

Garnish with a bit of chopped eggs or green and red onions. Serve with cocktail-size slices of rye bread.

Sweets — Patrick's Cranberry Experiment

My two children like good food, but only my son, Patrick, likes to cook it. After watching preparations for a couple of Thanksgiving meals, he announced before he could shave that he had developed his own recipe for the cranberries.

I was skeptical. But he nailed it. It's become our go-too Thanksgiving side dish.

Ingredients for 6 servings

Cranberries, fresh	1½ lb.
Orange juice	2 cups
Dark brown or Turbinado sugar	1 cup
Cinnamon	1 t
Clove, ground	1 t
Orange zest	1 T
Oranges or tangerines, peeled and seeded, sliced	2
Optional	
Sliced almonds	¼ cup

Wash berries.

In a heavy saucepan, add cranberries, orange juice, and sugar.

Bring to a full boil but avoid getting splashed as the sugar will burn deeply.

Add spices, zest and oranges or tangerines cut into small pieces (about six or seven per section). Stir well and continue to boil until berries pop open, usually about 5 minutes.

Carefully pour into bowl and cool.

Sweets Holiday Hazelnut Brittle

This recipe is adapted from a wonderful peanut brittle made by Mandy St. Amand and eagerly awaited each year by her lucky friends at the *St. Louis Post-Dispatch*. With hazelnuts being the most abundant nut in the Pacific Northwest, it seemed like a logical choice to make this substitution when we left St. Louis. Most agree it's almost as good as Mandy's brittle.

Above: Holiday Hazelnut Brittle. Photo by Jim Shearer

Ingredients for seven gift portions or a pound of snacks

Hazelnuts, crushed and toasted	2 cups
White sugar	2 cups
Light corn syrup	1 cup
Quality vanilla extract	½ t
Water	½ cup
Salted butter	1 cup
Nutmeg	1 t
Sea salt	¼ t
Baking soda	1 t

Preheat oven to 350 degrees.

Place nuts in a clean towel, tuck in all sides, and roll with a wooden dowel or rolling pin until the nuts are reduced to the desired size. Don't make the pieces too small.

Place on a dry baking pan and toast in the 350-degree oven until light brown and the aroma of roasted nuts fills the kitchen (about 14 to 16 minutes.). Stir every couple of minutes, using care not to burn. Remove from oven and set aside.

In a 3-quart heavy-bottom saucepan, combine sugar, corn syrup, vanilla extract, and water over a medium heat. Stir until dissolved, then add butter.

When temperature reaches 230 degrees on candy thermometer, begin stirring constantly, taking care to avoid getting splashed by the sugar mixture.

When the temperature reaches 280 degrees, carefully add the crushed nuts and nutmeg. The temperature will drop a bit at this point. Continue stirring until temperature reaches 305 degrees and nuts are honey golden in color.

Remove from heat and quickly stir in the baking soda, then pour onto a baking pan containing a silicon liner or parchment paper lightly coated in butter. Make sure the pan is on a flat, level surface and use a buttered spatula to spread mixture evenly. Sprinkle with sea salt.

Let cool at least 30 minutes, then crack into pieces. Eat or package well as treats.

To Be Continued in Your Kitchen

Andy's culinary adventures could have filled a book twice this size. But the clock ran out before he could write them all down. So many stories, he used to lament, so little time.

So savor every bite. These dishes taste better when shared with friends—and a side of good stories.

Above: Andrew Schneider. Photo by Paul Kitagaki Jr.

Acknowledgments

This book, like Andy's table, was made richer by friends.

Gifted editors and publishers Sandra Olivetti Martin and Bill Lambrecht pushed me to turn my aspiration of finishing Andy's cookbook into a reality. It would not have happened without them.

David McCumber, Jackie Koszczuk, Kimberly Marlowe Hartnett, and Neil McMahon, all terrific writers and editors, provided valuable feedback on early drafts.

Copy editor and author John McIntyre made sure we conformed to the rules of the English language.

Photographers Andrew Cutraro, Paul Kitagaki Jr., Vincent J. Musi, Patrick Schneider, and Kurt Wilson graciously allowed me to use their images. And brother Bob Best used his keen photographer's eye to edit the scores of food photos that Andy took.

Thank you, too, to the friends, family and friends-of-friends spanning 10 states from coast to coast who helped test the recipes. While Andy was good at making food, he was not always good about writing everything down that went in the pot or pan. Talented cooks Kim Anderson, Pamela Baker-Masson, Sonya Best, Terry Dragotta, Darrell Ehrlick, Gwen Florio, Tim Hartnett, Christian Masson, Hanna McDermott, Keven McDermott, Marcia Myers, Lore Postman, Cindy Shearer, Joe Sobczyk, and Elana Winsberg joined Kitagaki, Koszczuk, McCumber, and Musi to make sure nothing essential was missing.

As well as all these friends, designer Suzanne Shelden worked a miracle in making this book logical and beautiful.

Jacqueline Raines, Andy's feisty and beloved aunt, helped fill in details of his early years and inspires me constantly with her wicked smarts and sense of humor.

On Andy's behalf, thanks also go to all the people who shared their time, their wisdom, their techniques, their recipes and, of course, their stories.

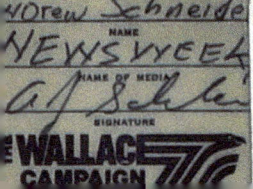

www.ingramcontent.com/pod-product-compliance
Lightning Source LLC
Chambersburg PA
CBHW061406010526
44119CB00011B/277